OUT OF THE BOX

Discover How God Is Big Enough For You

Ken Sylvia, MA

Lighthouse Global Publishing and PR

www.lighthouseglobalinc.com

ISBN: 978-1-950621-22-4 (ebook)

ISBN: 978-1-950621-23-1 (print)

Contents

Dedication

This book is dedicated to the men and women who mentored me and the young people who allowed me to mentor them.

While my son may never understand, this book is also dedicated to him because God has used him to make me more like Jesus.

Introduction

Early on in my marriage, I sat down with a mentor of mine over breakfast and discussed all the ironies and frustrations that go along with committing your life to someone else. It seems God not only had a plan in mind when creating the opposite sexes but also an incredible sense of humor. I forget why I was a little upset with my wife, but I sat across the table from this man, and he said to me, "You know, you're problem isn't your wife; it's you trying to force her onto your timetable." Essentially, this wise man was pointing out that my struggle with my wife at that moment was not that she was doing something I disagreed with or even that she was sinning, but that she wasn't "improving" in *my* approved time frame. I had an agenda for when and how she was supposed to change, and well, she was not falling in line with *my* plans.

Subconsciously, I was trying to control my wife, and I don't know about you, but it never seems to work out very well when we try to force people into our agendas. I never intended to, and I would never want to harm my wife, but the truth is that I was attempting to insert my will, expectations, and desires into her life. Relationships, especially marriage, are so tricky because often our actions (or lack of actions) impact others and vice versa. Through this particular experience, I realized that *my* personal issues have influenced how much I try to grab hold of my wife's life out of fear and insecurity that something bad might happen *to me*, or that she's not close enough to God *for me*, or that she doesn't care enough *about me*. I can only speak for myself, but I've come to realize that my so-called "control issues" stem from *Me*.

This got me thinking about how much of life's problems stem from our attempt to control. Have you ever thought of that? I mean, it seems that the primary reason we get into arguments is because people don't see our way, which obviously we all know is *the* "right" way (sarcasm inserted here).

Negative manipulation tactics seem to be the new method of casual communication. Take a look out the window – or rather down at your phone – and within one scroll, you'll easily hear and see how shameful you are for not having the "correct" opinion at that particular moment. Flip through the news channels to see what "shocking revelations" corporations have come under fire - this time - for laundering, extorting, cheating, monopolizing, etc. If you watch enough news, then you'll quickly learn that you must pick a side, take up a cause, or cast all critical thinking to the wind, or else face extreme criticism. Controlling people is as easy as defining only one correct answer, even if it's wrong.

As a self-proclaimed nerd, I love trying to understand why things are the way that they are. What can really be gained from all the manipulative tactics in the world, in our relationships, or even in our minds? Is it fame and fortune? Is it fear, lust, selfishness, or some other dark trait lurking in the shadows? Or, could it be as simple as having a God-complex? Regardless of the underlying reason for control, there's a bigger picture that I invite you to explore with me: God just isn't big enough.

The control issues that we struggle with or perhaps even pride ourselves on stem from a misguided perspective of who God is and what God is. For example, have you ever thought to yourself, "If *I* am having all these problems, then can God really be as good and strong and loving as He says He is?" If somehow we conclude that He is not, then we must be god in order to address whatever it is in front of us. How easy, almost natural, is it to take our preconceived, short-sighted, limited views of God and place Him nicely into the box of our choosing? We select the wrapping paper, bows, and décor and feel good about how awesome the god in our box is. We consider ourselves experts and brag about how well designed the box is, and much like professional Christmas gift wrapping, the flawless "tape-job" to ensure smooth, clear lines. That is until the god in our box doesn't act like the God we think we know. As the paper rips, cardboard breaks, and contents spill out, we then respond angrily or even walk away because the god we thought we had figured out, let us down.

Ultimately, this book is part of my story, but it is also my attempt to help people who – just like me – struggle with God-complex. Whether you are struggling with a friend or relative, or whether you are struggling with a major decision in life, I have written this book so that I might share what God has taught me about Himself and about my *self* in this world. I do not claim that this is a "fix-all" type of self-help book; rather I believe that this is designed to help you re-think God's goodness, greatness, love, power, strength, and person. After all, He is the only person to raise the dead to life, and there's no box for that.

I write this with the hope and prayer that God would use my story to help you leave space in your heart, mind, and soul for God to be as big as you'll let Him. Working with teenage youth for nearly 20 years, I have painstakingly watched them wrestle and struggle with who has the most control in their relationships. With girlfriends/boyfriends who let them down, parents who just don't understand, teachers who are "mean," and friends who pressure them, even their most peaceful of days contain a weight of chaos that feels like God isn't what the stories make Him out to be. However, this perspective is often formulated from experience, and modern psychology reinforces the idea that we view God based upon our early relationships. Therefore, I hope and pray that this will help you to pause in the midst of the storm, evaluate what you think you know, and help you to recognize that God *really is* big enough to engage your life, your problems, your fears, your insecurities and yes... even your control. Consider your preconceived beliefs, the reasonings behind those beliefs, and I invite you into the journey of discovering the "bigger picture". God really is big enough.

Let God out of the box...

CONTROL–
EXERCISING COMMAND

CHAPTER 1

Control-Exercising Command

I love the *X-Men* movies. In fact, not long ago, I had the urge to have an X-Men marathon from start to finish. If you are unfamiliar with the X-Men series, don't admit that to anyone, and Google how to rent them. But, I digress. In short, Charles Xavier – or Professor X – has the superpower of mind control and the ability to read other people's thoughts. He uses "Cerebro" in order to locate, track and communicate with mutants and humans. He is not only the leader of the X-Men, but one of the most powerful of the mutants. As I was watching the saga, I couldn't help but wonder how many people dream of having his powers. I know if I had his powers, I would be writing an entirely different book, or perhaps wouldn't be writing at all, and would just read your mind and charge you for that.

We may never verbally say it, but we think about it: "If only I could really know what he was thinking." "If only I could make her see what I'm really feeling." "I wish I could make him stop making such bad decisions." The power of knowing others thoughts can be so intoxicating because interacting with other humans can be a very painful and difficult process. If only we could infiltrate and influence those thoughts, it would make it so much easier on us, and their lives would be so much better having our help! Or, so we tell ourselves.

Each of us has our own unique personalities, opinions, life experiences, insecurities, filters, communication styles, and Facebook quiz results. If you haven't noticed, all of these things combine to make each of us very different from one another. These differences cause conflict along with the accompanying feelings of frustration and can lead us toward trying to control the person, thing, or situation that is stirring up these feelings. Surely, even right now, you can think of that situation with your spouse, child, or co-worker that's left you feeling fed-up, tired, lost, confused, or at your wit's end.

One would think that "control" is simple to describe. Most people would say that it has to deal with simply being in charge, but on a foundational level, "control" is a way of exercising command over someone or something. It's not "just to be in charge," but to have complete power, authority, and superiority over that person or thing. For example, Professor X uses "Cerebro" for the greater good, so that all of the mutants and the humans can live in harmony. It's still manipulation, but at least it feels better. On the other hand, Magneto uses Cerebro to exercise command over the humans and to kill them, while Striker replicates Cerebro so that he can kill all the mutants.

Just like in the movies, the real world is never simple and easy. Consider how the government exercises command over how much tax we pay, businesses exercise command over goods and services, and we attempt to exercise command over our family pets. Although, I am convinced my dog only allows me to think I have such power, and in reality, am subjected to her mercy. I don't know about you, but it sometimes feels like I'm riding the wave of the powers-at-be craving just one moment of autonomy.

Regardless of our reasoning for why we attempt to control what is around us, or even to what extent we attempt to control, we must recognize that it is a very real issue, and we must address it head-on if we are to experience life to the fullest (see John 10: 10). *Boundaries*, a popular book by Drs. Henry Cloud & John Townsend, is one of my favorites. The subtitle of the book is "When to Say Yes, How to Say No, To Take Control of Your Life." If you have yet to read this book, I highly recommend that you pick it up or purchase the audio version so you can listen to it on the go, because appropriate, healthy boundaries are very pertinent to the topic at hand.

Appropriate, healthy boundaries are what keep us safe, secure, healthy, and functioning properly. They are what guide us to push harmful things away and bring helpful things near. Having a lack of healthy boundaries in our lives can lead us to feel out of control, which ironically leads us to attempt to control. We can feel at times like the earth's axis rests on our shoulders, and if we fail at being perfect, then all humanity will be sucked into some black hole (or maybe that's just me). We can feel like the only way to protect ourselves is through manipulation, never saying "no" to someone else or being involved in every little thing because, well... we aren't really sure why.

Creating healthy boundaries in our lives helps us to make decisions and live in such a way as to "take control" in a positive, healthy way over Me, Myself, and I. However, if you are like me – even in the least bit – you are already asking, "What about when things are out of control, and no quantity or quality of boundaries will help fix it?" Maybe you have experienced a situation – or are currently in a situation – when you threw your hands up in the air screaming, "That's it! I can't do it! I've had enough!" If you are like me, you are already getting a knot in your stomach at the very thought of allowing the world around you to be a little out of order. I hate feeling out of control, but have you ever dealt with someone who just seems to continue to cause you heartache no matter how much you pray, cry and get counseling? Taking control, whatever the heck that is, just doesn't seem to work sometimes, or ever.

I believe that the truth of the matter is if we are completely honest with ourselves, we really don't have all that much control in our lives. Exercising command over our own life decisions is hard enough, let alone trying to do so with others around us. Boundaries are about making decisions that allow *you* to better manage *your* life, but they will not help you to fix any and every situation so that everything and everyone obey your every command. There has to be a balance of appropriate boundaries while acknowledging our lack of control over every situation that life may bring us.

However, in the spirit of reflection, think of a time when you have been "in charge"? I don't want you to just think of a time when you were the "point person" or "manager", but when you really did control the outcome. Now consider this: how did it make you feel when you were exercising command? What were the circumstances? Did any conflicts arise out of this? How much control did you really have? How much of it was simply perceived?

Now I want you to stop and think about a time when you were the subject of someone else's control. Consider all the nuance of that circumstance. Who was involved? What percentage of the equation were you responsible for? How did it make you feel? How did you respond, and what options did you have?

Perhaps the greatest of all struggles over who gets to be ultimately in control is that of the average teenager and parent. I love my mother, she has a kind and generous heart, and I know that she would be willing to sacrifice herself for the sake of me and my siblings. However, maybe you can empathize with me when I say that my mom had to have her way. There were no ifs, ands, or buts. In fact, even if her way did not make as much sense as my way, or if I could prove my way was a better way, I had two options: 1) jump on the mommy train, or 2) "hear" about it, which was going to be a very unpleasant experience.

The teenage years are the toughest of them all because these creatures are stuck between *not* being children anymore, but also *not* yet fully independent as adults.

Children need the security and protection of knowing that their parents are "in control", yet human nature is thus that we do not want to be controlled. This explains why you want to pull your hair out some days if you are a parent. However, maybe you can relate to a time when your parents either didn't have an answer or weren't available to you in a time of crisis. Those experiences can leave us feeling helpless and abandoned, and can trigger a drive to "never feel that again".

The feeling of security is foundationally important for a child's development in the early years. Feeling loved in a stable environment is crucial for healthy growth of the mind and emotions, but especially for the processing of relationships. As children grow, painful experiences follow. I've met with hundreds of teenagers who look back at painful moments in their lives, but who didn't have that sense of security. So, by the time they are in high school, for example, I found myself trying to help them navigate the need to depend on adults around them, but also their lack of trust for these same adults – I being one of them.

I watched many of these young people push and challenge, sometimes just out of desperation, in an attempt to feel like they have autonomy. Of course, the natural response many times was to employ manipulation against their attitude or misbehavior, which made the adults feel better but was hardly productive or effective long-term. Personally, despite the head-knowledge that I have of my mom's love for me, there were times growing up when her attempts at exercising control over my life left me feeling helpless, cornered, emasculated, and defeated. *Some* teenagers react to this kind of behavior by simply giving up as a way of saying, "Fine, you win, do whatever you want, I'll quit trying to have autonomy, you are superior." However, I'm not "some", so needless to say my mother and I quarreled often and intensely over whom got the "W" at the end of the match.

After I began following Christ as a mid-teen, I sought out some professional counseling when a mentor of mine encouraged me with, "You're messed up, you need help!" It actually became the focal point of some of our inside jokes. The original purpose for my sometimes frequent visits to "Tell Me About That" stemmed from my inability to manage my outbursts. I could not identify how I felt, which left me feeling angry, which usually resulted in something being broken. I realized that if I truly wanted to follow Jesus, and that if I truly wanted to be different, then the whole "ticking time bomb" thing was going to have to change.

You see, the way that you "won" (or were heard) in my household was to throw something, or yell louder than your opponent, which usually ended up being mom. I still joke with one of my siblings about the Great Kitchen Debacle. My mother and I began to have a conversation over something, which turned into a difference of opinion and a desire to explain, which turned into more of a conflict, so I began to practice all my newfound communication "skills" through counseling. However, my attempts at proper communication seemed pointless as my mother became very accusatory, defensive, and loud. This ultimately led to my inability to manage or cope effectively and also a chair flying across the room while I screamed, "You're not listening!" Needless to say, that tactic didn't actually help my case, but it's how I felt I could still have autonomy at that moment.

Physical aggression and shouting were the two ways that I learned to exercise command over a situation. These were the only two ways that I knew how to "win". However, as I began to grow and change, I knew Jesus was calling me to be more than some person who dominated everything via aggression or extreme volume, but I didn't know how to be different so I swung to the other side of the pendulum. This left me deliberately suppressing any public display of emotion, shoving what I could down, and doing whatever necessary to maintain the façade of control.

I was just showing a different kind of emotion, and this moderate depression left me feeling voiceless, not wanting to explode, but not yet knowing how to practically, respectfully, lovingly speaking up. I simply could not communicate in the midst of strong opinion, tension or conflict, especially if that conflict involved a woman. In fact, my wife and I struggled with this when we were dating because I would get mad over something she said or did, even if it was ridiculous and silly, and I would avoid her in a passive-aggressive manner for sometimes days at a time. By the grace of God, and with hours of therapy and prayer, I have come such a long way, but I share this to show the impact that external factors can have on how we exercise command.

I had *learned* some things about women growing up: 1) they are always right... therefore, don't bother talking with them; 2) They will emasculate you at all cost... therefore, you must fight them to protect your dignity, and 3) They have no respect for men... therefore, what you think and feel don't really matter to them anyway. I honestly thought that my wife would be like "all the other women" I had experienced with no respect, no regard, and hell-bent on emasculating me (despite my deep love and affection for her). I didn't want to hurt her or interact with her as I had my mom, so I figured the best way to control situations where I felt out of control was to act in a passive-aggressive manner. This was my way of "exercising command", and communicating, "I'll show you! You're not going to win!" But this attitude left neither of us winning.

Let me stop and say that I have grown up quite a bit since that time, and I do not believe that all women are evil emasculators. God has healed me from some of those wounds, and I have incredible women in my life that I am so grateful for who have helped me to process, but this is a continual work for me. Besides being blessed with Godly women in my life who are not like "all the other women", my wife strives to protect my dignity and honor, and demonstrate respect while I strive to open up to her with what I'm really feeling and thinking so that I don't randomly blow up on her... or shut her out.

We must understand that this desire to exercise command may be a more difficult struggle for some more than others and that this process will be different for every person, but we have to start somewhere in order to move forward. I believe in the truth of Philippians 4:13, that we can do all things through Christ who gives us strength. My encouragement to you is to start by going before the throne of God, admitting where you are at in this process, and asking Him to give you strength, humility, and a realization of your brokenness as you begin – or even continue on – in this journey.

Struggling for Authority

I believe that our desire to exercise command stems from our root desire to have ultimate authority. It does not matter who we are, where we have come from, or what personality type we have, we want to have authority. The moment that sin entered into the world, we began fighting to be like God. I'm not trying to insinuate that we want to have equality with God as Supreme Ruler, but I am suggesting that in our brokenness we knee-jerk for the steering wheel. For example, do we really mean it when we pray "Your will be done, on earth as it is in Heaven", or do we really mean "Your will be done, as long as it fits within my whims, wishes, and will. Amen."

There are different levels of authority. For example, children are to obey and respect the authority of the parents, and parents are to obey and respect the authority of the law, and the (United States') government is designed to obey the will of the people, and on and on we go. I believe that we were created to be under authority and that it is within our DNA to follow, but the million-dollar question is, "Who is ultimately in charge?" Who has supreme authority? Who are we suppose to follow? Who gives "so and so" or "such and such person" the right to exercise command over me and my life?

Whether we realize it or not, or whether we would like to accept it or not, these questions are at the root of our underlying motivations for controlling people and/or situations. For example, my previous mentor understood this and every now and again would poke at me, "I bet you can't... (fill in the blank)." Since I tend to be competitive in nature, I would react to him in a way that communicated, "I'll show you!". Ultimately, this is my way of saying, "You're wrong, I'm in control, I'm the winner!" Even though I knew he was in charge, there is still that inner struggle over who rules me, or who I allow to rule me (which we will talk about more in-depth later on).

The Bible traces this struggle for personal authority all the way back in the Heavenly realms when Lucifer (also known as Satan, the Enemy) thought to himself that he had enough authority to exceed the ranks of the Great I AM. I like the New King James Version of Isaiah 14:11-15...

11 Your pomp is brought down to Sheol, And the sound of your stringed instruments; The maggot is spread under you, And worms cover you.' 12 "How you are fallen from heaven, O Lucifer, son of the morning! How you are cut down to the ground, You who weakened the nations! 13 For you have said in your heart: 'I will ascend into heaven, I will exalt my throne above the stars of God; I will also sit on the mount of the congregation On the farthest sides of the north; 14 I will ascend above the heights of the clouds, I will be like the Most High.' 15 Yet you shall be brought down to Sheol, To the lowest depths of the Pit.

I find it interesting that this passage alludes to the simple thought and attitude of Lucifer. It would seem that he does not go to God, make a case, have a conversation, and then get into a full-blown argument about who is actually more powerful. Instead, Lucifer's problem was that he had a self-exalted *attitude*, which is stated in verse 13: "For you have said in your heart..." So, it seems that the overall struggle for authority does not begin with external rewards such as being the president or demanding when the child's chores will be completed, but instead the struggle for authority begins within the attitudes of our hearts.

Take a moment to think about your attitudes in any past or current conflicts you might be experiencing. Is there an unmet or unsatisfied expectation? Is there a fear that haunts your mind? Or perhaps, like Lucifer, do you have a sense of entitlement or self-pride? I understand these questions are direct and intense, but if we are going to experience life to the fullest, that Jesus promises through a relationship with Him, then we must lay our thoughts, feelings, and control at His feet. We have to choose, from our heart, to allow Him to dig deep into our hearts and minds to cleanse and purify us so that we might better reflect His glory.

This struggle over control continues in Genesis when Adam and Eve are tempted by the serpent, sin against God, and are then cast out of the Garden of Eden. The New Living Translation tells the story of Genesis 3:1-13 quite nicely:

1 Now the serpent was the shrewdest of all the creatures the LORD God had made. "Really?" he asked the woman. "Did God really say you must not eat any of the fruit in the garden?" *2* "Of course we may eat it," the woman told him. *3* "It's only the fruit from the tree at the center of the garden that we are not allowed to eat. God says we must not eat it or even touch it, or we will die." *4* "You won't die!" the serpent hissed. *5* "God knows that your eyes will be opened when you eat it. You will become just like God, knowing everything, both good and evil." *6* The woman was convinced. The fruit looked so fresh and delicious, and it would make her so wise! So she ate some of the fruit. She also gave some to her husband, who was with her. Then he ate it, too. *7* At that moment, their eyes were opened, and they suddenly felt shame at their nakedness. So they strung fig leaves together around their hips to cover themselves. *8* Toward evening they heard the LORD God walking about in the garden, so they hid themselves among the trees. *9* The LORD God called to Adam, "Where are you?" *10* He replied, "I heard you, so I hid. I was afraid because I was naked." *11* "Who told you that you were naked?" the LORD God asked. "Have you eaten the fruit I commanded you not to eat?" *12* "Yes," Adam admitted, "but it was the woman you gave me who brought me the fruit, and I ate it." *13* Then the LORD God asked the woman, "How could you do such a thing?""The serpent tricked me," she replied. "That's why I ate it."

The serpent (or Satan) convinces Adam and Eve to disobey God through his trickery in this passage, and God holds all three of them responsible for their actions. However, I have often wondered if God simply gave us the shortened version of the story. After all, Adam and

Eve were willing to disobey God after one conversation with a serpent? I guess that just doesn't make sense to me. But, what if - for the sake of imagination - Eve had pondered and thought and "said in her heart... I will be like the Most High," just as Lucifer did in the Isaiah passage? What if prior to this conversation with the serpent she had become convinced in her heart that there was something better for her, that God was holding out on her and that somehow the fruit from this sacred tree would free her, giving her ultimate control and God-like status?

As Proverbs 4:23 tells us it is out of our hearts that words and actions follow. Reflecting, evaluating, and exercising command over the heart is the ultimate battle we face.

The balance of validating whatever it is we have going on internally with regulating those things that do not align with the goodness of God will forever be the ultimate human condition.

KEN SYLVIA

The balance of validating whatever it is we have going on internally with regulating those things that do not align with the goodness of God will forever be the ultimate human condition.

The War with Our Minds

We must be aware that Satan is in an all-out war with our minds. It's not just what we think about, but how we think about things. Having a regulated internal process is what led Joseph to flee from sin, David to approach the giant, and Jesus to choose the cross. These examples all demonstrate the discipline of exercising command over their internal processes. They were each presented with a predicament that had some level of temptation, fear, pain, or threat and yet controlled the direction of their minds and hearts.

If Satan can trick us into thinking that God's will for our lives is somehow keeping us from goodness, then we become like Eve, sucked into the abysmal pit of the Devil's lies that God is simply a fraud making false promises. Imagine if Joseph had said, "No one will ever find out", or if David reasoned, "It's not my fight", or Jesus said, "If I'm truly your son, you won't ask this of me." I find it interesting that not only do Adam and Eve die, but everyone after them, even though you and I had no say in the matter. While they didn't die immediately, I do find it intriguing that the lifespans of those in the Bible become incrementally shorter as the Great Story unfolds.

They not only physically die, but experience spiritual death as well. Satan blatantly lied to Adam and Eve, but fooled them by wrapping it up in a nice package, with a pretty bow and a sparkly nametag, and they become lost in some fantasy that God was holding out on them. They took the bait, and got pulled into never-ending strife of wanting what they had pre-fruit bite, but with the hopeless attempt of doing it on their own. They – along with you and I – quickly discovered that they will never have the fullness of life they desired through their own control.

I wonder if this is where the saying, "You don't know what you've got until it's gone" comes from. Adam and Eve had it perfect! They had every want and need satisfied. They walked, in person, with the God of the Universe! Adam even got to name all the animals! Pain, sickness, fear, worry, anxiety, stress, and the need to control were more alien than aliens themselves. Yet, somehow in the depths of their hearts, they lost contentment with where God had placed them. Their hearts craved more, and their minds wandered down a path with all the road signs showing images of the grass being greener on the other side.

The early Church leaders clearly understood the battle of the heart and mind as the old ways and the new ways were battling each other out. In fact, the Church of Ephesus was in such need of a reminder that the apostle Paul carves out part of his book to them instructing them to be ready for battle, wearing the armor of God, including the "helmet of Salvation" (Ephesians 6:17). Obviously, the helmet is a defensive piece of armor. It is a thick piece of metal, that while often decorated to give off some kind of fashion statement, has a primary function of ensuring that the control center of the body stays intact.

I am no Jedi Master theologian, but it would make sense that Paul understood the defensive nature of the helmet, and that is why he chose to call it the helmet of Salvation. The battle within our minds to focus on what is right and true is ongoing, real, and at times wearisome. As a Christian – follower of Christ – my identity is first and foremost rooted in my Salvation through Christ Jesus. Our thought control center must stay grounded in salvation. If that at any point comes into question, then my foundation for life ceases to exist.

Salvation at a foundational, essential level is the ultimate, supreme goodness of the person and the work of Jesus Christ the Son of God (see John 14:6). Wearing this protective piece of equipment allows us to remain in the thought and knowledge of this goodness, experiencing an inexplicable joy even when life's not fair, and the pain of brokenness is very real. Adam and Eve didn't just pay the penalty of death when they acted on the suspicion that God was withholding something from them, but they paid through the loss of walking in the goodness of God.

Earlier in the New Testament, the apostle Paul tells the Roman church to be "transformed by the renewing of your mind" so that they can "test and approve what God's will is – His good, pleasing, and perfect will" (Romans 12:2). This further shows that Paul was personally familiar with the battle within the mind. But, pause for a second and imagine being Paul, formerly Saul who is so convinced he's right about being on fire for God that he travels the countryside approving the murder of people who simply have a belief that Jesus was God. Then, one day as he was journeying along, lights flash, voices boom, and scales cover his eyes. The rest is history as God transforms him into a hero and martyr of early Christianity.

Let's examine the four specific pieces of this verse for the sake of the topic at hand: 1) renewing the mind, 2) being transformed, 3) testing and approving of God's will, and 4) His good will.

First, renewing the mind seems to be a loaded phrase. How does one go about renewing the mind? Do you take a good nap, visit a Christian yoga class, or perhaps read a good fiction novel out of the local Christian bookstore that makes you ponder the love of Jesus? Somehow, I don't think that is what Paul was referencing when he wrote this. In the simplest of terms, Paul was referring to the old, sinful nature versus the new spirit-filled nature. Renewing our minds must start with reevaluating who Jesus Christ is to us, and how Jesus Christ functions as the Holy Spirit inside of us. In essence, what we think about God will affect how we act toward Him, and others.

Let's stop for a second and rewrite this story of Adam and Eve conversing in the Garden of Eden just for fun. Imagine the scene: birds are chirping, a slight breeze makes the leaves conduct a calm, serene melody, while Adam and Eve walk hand-in-hand, stopping to give a romantic kiss in front of a small waterfall that fills a small heart-shaped pond. Just outside of this pond is a large, robust, and very fruitful tree which has a sign posted in the Holy, Ancient language:

"This is the Tree of Knowledge. Please do not eat from this tree, or you will die. All Creation appreciates your obedience."
~With Love, Your Creator.

Now, imagine Adam and Eve are drying off just outside the shade of this tree, laying in the grass, soaking up the sun, casually leaning back, watching the ducks clean themselves in the pond while fish jump out of the water every now and again. Being man, Adam gets bored real easy and goes to look for some stones to skip across the pond while Eve situates herself under the shade of this giant tree to take a nap.

After a few moments, Adam looks over and sees the serpent crawling out of the giant tree to strike up a conversation with Eve, so he jogs on over to see what the conversation is all about. After discussing the weather, politics, and favorite desserts, Satan suggests a new fruit pie he wants Adam and Eve to try... and how different would this story end if Adam and Eve stopped to read the part of the sign that says, "With Love, Your Creator"?

Unfortunately, this is not how the conversation ended. Instead, our ancestors' minds were left stagnant, stuck on the lust in front of them. They failed to critically think, let alone throw a flag on the play, and cry out, "Creator! This slithery thing over here says that we can be like you if we eat from the tree, what's the deal here?" The lack of renewal leaves generations of brokenness, pain, and sin, and not because Satan is an evil tempter – though that is true – but because Adam and Eve bought the lie that God really isn't good enough.

Rather than exercising command over their thoughts, clinging to the experience and truth of God's perfect presence in the Garden, they gave in to the enticement of something more. The foundation of their actions was rooted in mistrust in their Creator, and their beliefs led them down a road of unintended suffering. Being transformed requires a constant foundation check. Daily, hourly, constantly practicing the art of catching your thoughts, and pointing them toward The Way, The Truth, and The Life (John 14:6).

Being transformed is the process by which "who" we are is altered at the soul level. Following Christ requires surrender and sacrifice, and as we do that – specifically in our minds as the starting place of our emotional or behavioral responses – we must check the routes of our neural pathways. Practicing critical thinking is incredibly difficult because enough information has to be acquired in order to complete the puzzle. At the same time, critical thinking is absolutely crucial because it trains the brain to analyze all the different possibilities like, "Is God really holding out on me? Does He not want me to be like Him, or is He trying to protect me from something I cannot see?" Something mysterious happens to "who" we are as God reveals a bigger picture. Instead of relating to God as a selfish deity holding out on us, we relate to Him as a Loving Father giving us free will transforms our relationship with Him.

This then raises the ambition to test and approve God's will. If walking in freedom and peace with the Creator is so desirable, then it would logically follow that we will do whatever it takes to do so. However, while I don't want to get caught up in semantics, we aren't talking about just "questioning" things. No, we are talking about digging in, diving to the depths, and searching for that tiny detail that could illuminate a slightly deeper truth into God's person and plan. Creating a habit and discipline of testing the thought, and being confident that it aligns with Who He is and what He accomplished in history transforms us into a more accurate reflection of Him.

Finally, who God is, is Good. So His will then, is good. Renewing our minds, being transformed, testing, and approving His will all culminates into the revelation that HE... IS... GOOD! It is impossible for God to be anything other than good. Any line of thinking that comes to a conclusion that God is not so, means we have to slam the clutch in, throw it into reverse, and back it up to see where along the road we made the wrong turn.

The Real Challenge

Ultimately, the issue of the Forbidden Fruit comes down to who is in charge. Ever since Adam and Eve walked the earth, humanity has been fighting God over control of their lives. If we are honest, we struggle with this every day. Are we truly willing to allow God to exercise command over our lives? Are we willing to actively listen to His perfect will and then act accordingly? After all, the only real request God has of us is to believe in His goodness and to obey His will. These are basic requests, but require that we submit ourselves and orient ourselves under "Him".

The consequences for Adam and Eve's lack of trust (or disbelief) in who and what God is resulted in hard labor, pain, loss, grief, sadness, shame, and death. Adam and Eve hurt themselves and all of creation by trying to exercise command over the situation. Genesis 3:7 shows that they became *aware* that they were naked, resulting in shame, which was an entirely new emotion not included in the original design of Man. I could not imagine living as Adam and Eve in Heaven on planet Earth, knowing nothing of "evil" to suddenly experiencing the sickening feeling of sin requiring hiding in shame as the only remedy.

Perhaps you or I cannot relate to Adam and Eve's specific situation, but can you relate to that sudden nauseous feeling after really blowing it? Adam and Eve paid a much greater price than they originally anticipated by attempting to take control of what was "right and wrong". In fact, isn't that how it usually works out? We think that the activity which we are about to participate in, whatever it may be, will have a much greater yield than cost. Adam and Eve's decision to deliberately distrust God resulted in the breaking of a perfect, harmonious relationship between their Creator and each other.

Selfishness is about what we want when we want it and how we want it because it is all about "me" (or in your case, "you"). If "me" (or "you") isn't getting our way, we knee-jerk react to think that God's holding out.

Which of course means that the only possible solution is for us to overtake the command post because only we know what we really need (or at least that's what we tell ourselves). However, we forget that life doesn't exist in a vacuum, and that life consists of dynamic relationships, and that our actions and decisions can have significant consequences for our immediate families, close friends, future generations, and even random strangers. Think about it, with the single bite of a fruit, first by Eve and then by Adam, hundreds of generations have experienced brokenness in relationship between each other and God all because they just *had to have* the knowledge of "good and evil"... ironically leading to not only a literal but also metaphorical death. They couldn't foresee that there was a reason God was telling them "no".

Responsibility

Perhaps something that we often overlook is that with "command" comes "responsibility". You can ask any CEO, senior pastor, manager, coach, captain, or parent, and they will tell you that they feel responsible for those within their command. They have a deep sense of duty that leads them to think, "I have to be in control of our operations, or else..." As parents of a special needs child, my wife and I often wrestle with being ultra-careful, doing all the "right things", and trying to figure out what's wrong, but in our most vulnerable, helpless times surrender to the ultimate truth that my amazing little boy really belongs to His Heavenly Father, and I'm just the guy who gets to help oversee his time on earth. I understand that while I'm very much responsible for his life now, I'm not ultimately in control of what happens to him now or in eternity.

Adam and Eve made a decision, exercising command over that stupid fruit, but then were not able (or willing) to take responsibility for their actions. Assuming their selfish actions could only possibly result in positive outcomes, they were unable to address the failure as they cowered in shame. Allowing God to exercise command over our lives does not mean that we brush off any responsibility for our actions, as if to imply we are merely puppets in a cruel stage play. Rather, placing God in His rightful place in our lives enhances our awareness of personal responsibility because we are brutally aware of our duty, accountability, and calling to Him.

Genesis 3:6 describes the scene: The serpent makes a strong closing argument that Eve would actually benefit from taking a bite of the beautiful, tasty-looking fruit (which I'm assuming had to be a pluot), and after sinking her incisors into the delicious, mouthwatering snack, she hands it to her husband "who was with her". Now, I do not know at what point Adam joined Eve and the serpent in the conversation, but the Good Book implies that he knew exactly what he was doing when he stood, watched, listened, then received the fruit. In fact, I would argue with obvious literary license that the first sin was done by Adam when he failed to lovingly speak truth to his wife. After all, didn't God give Adam the direct command to not eat the fruit? The serpent preyed upon Eve and Adam failed to protect her, and one could even argue, abandon her. This is only proof of what a beautiful naked woman with food can do to a man's thinking capacity (joking, kind of).

In my humble opinion, there was nothing significant about the fruit. Maybe it was an apple or maybe it was a grapefruit, some say it could have been a pomegranate, fig, or pear, but the real "fruit" was in God's command to not eat it. Adam and Eve blatantly disobeyed God's will and that decision has had grave consequences ever since. Our ancestors failed to take responsibility for obeying the original command given by God. This lack of personal responsibility, first to the Lord, second to each other, led to the pain we all now experience in our relationships.

Later that evening, God steps down for His nightly stroll, and after making it clear that He knew they were hiding, Adam pops out from behind the bushes, and with the stiffest of pointed index finger screams, "She made me do it!" followed by Eve's screech, "That slimy thing over there made me do it!" Which, of course, the serpent loses its legs and its "best friends forever" status with Eve, but I digress. Taking control as Adam and Eve did threw humanity into a downward spiral of the well known blame-game. It is a rare occasion to find people who have the strength and determination to admit to their sin and wrongs, to own up to them, and take responsibility for their actions (including the consequences of those actions). However, taking ownership allows us to reflect more of God's goodness.

The instant awareness of the knowledge of good and bad led Adam to step off of his leadership post, to look down upon his wife in bitterness, and led Eve to have the temptation to rule over her husband, attempting to control his every step. Neither of them owned up and confessed to their actions. Their shame in themselves was so overwhelming, the only thing they could control was the direction their finger pointed. Shame essentially says, "*Who* you are is bad." But, attempting to divert the attention off of ourselves only creates more destruction. Victory over this shame can only be accomplished by humbling ourselves and owning up to what we've done.

God never changed *who* He was in the story of Adam and Eve. Rather, their actions led to a change in *how* they viewed and interacted with God. The result of their disobedience was being closed off from the Garden. While God carried out the result of their sin, their actions resulted in the consequence of having to be removed from the Garden. This is important to grasp because God continued to be good. In fact, it was good to remove them from a place of perfection, when they ceased to be perfect.

How often have you heard someone in a relationship say, "Well, I wouldn't have done 'this' *if you* weren't so 'that'?" Or how many times have you heard someone make up an excuse for why they were late, why they used foul language, why they didn't follow through with commitments, or countless other scenarios. These are attempts to rid ourselves of the shame because of the "this" or "that" which causes us to believe something very bad about ourselves... and so the excuses start flying! Think about it for a second, even if Eve had a gun to Adam's head, he still has a decision to make: be shot or eat the fruit. However, do you see the missing verse? You know, the verse where Adam thinks through his decision, acts, and then takes responsibility before the Lord to own up to what he did. Exactly, it is a missing verse because that never happened! No, instead he too took a bite, their eyes both opened and their shame was so deep they began pointing the finger in anger, bitterness, and resentment.

This is the deception of thinking that we can take control and exercise command over our lives. When we do this, we must take responsibility for it, which is a responsibility most of us are unable to bear. Therefore, we must confess our sin, humble ourselves before our loving Father, and accept the gift of forgiveness that only He can offer.

My wife and I argue. In fact, are there any married couples who don't? If you know of a couple who doesn't argue, then I argue that they need therapy because someone is obviously avoiding something in the relationship. But, since my wife and I argue, we have made a commitment to do these three things: 1) be honest with how we feel about the situation, as to avoid shaming the other person, 2) take responsibility for our individual percentage of the problem, whether it be 5% or 95%, and 3) humbly apologize for the wrong done, specifically naming what it was. Imagine if Adam had said, "Eve, I let you down, there's no excuse, it's my fault for not protecting you from the Enemy", or if Eve said, "Adam, you told me about this tree, and I doubted you." I guess we'll never know if that would have changed the impact on eternity. In short, people simply want to know that the other person in the relationship is willing to take responsibility for his or her actions, and to do whatever it takes to make it right. This attitude honors God and places Him in His rightful place of authority over our lives as it models Biblical living.

HE'S BIG, JUST NOT BIG ENOUGH

CHAPTER 2

LIE #1: GOD NEEDS ME.

God is Big, Just Not Big Enough

Lie #1: God needs me to intervene

As we looked at in chapter one, Adam and Eve had an issue with trusting the supreme goodness of God and His perfect will. They took the bait and bought into the lie that God was not big enough to give them exactly what they wanted and needed. They were sold on the deception that God was holding out on them because He didn't want them to be like Him, knowing the difference between good and evil. They sought equality to God without truly understanding the unforeseen negative consequences of what that would entail.

You can crack open almost any psychology or religious book to know that most of the people in the world believe there is some sort of God. Whether this God has the name Jesus Christ or not is where the arguments arise, but the bottom line is that throughout history and many cultures there has been the major belief that there's a higher power, or an un-created Being (or beings according to some philosophies and religions). This "higher power" has always acted to control or dominate the world in which we live. From nature around us to sexuality to stars in the sky, Mankind has attempted to try and figure out this indescribable supremacy. This has ultimately been where the difference of opinions take root: the function and role of "God" in our lives. Some might consider Him to be a loving Father who wants to keep us safe and happy, while others might see Him as a just God who sits on high ready to punish those who disobey Him, or maybe even a busy God who doesn't have enough time to get off His backside and help out with the troubles and calamities that life throws at us.

This is where as limited, frail flesh we shove God into a box. However, please do not misunderstand me. Many of us will create really big, nice, glamorous boxes to help us feel like we have a better understanding. I mean, look at how big of a box I built for God to fit in! I am so much closer to Him, far more spiritual because I have a deeper knowledge of who He really is. Psychologically, this is absolutely normal. Our finite brains' knee-jerk reaction is to make sense of the world around us, and when we can't, we create constructs and parameters to help our limited understanding make better sense. The problem is that faith by definition demands we crack open that box and adjust our limited parameters. For example, "Is God really big enough for (fill in the blank)". Let's assume the answer is "yes", but perhaps He doesn't answer "yes". Does that then mean God is not big enough, or does it mean we limited God to only a limited set of options, when in fact His story for our lives is much bigger than that?

Have you ever thought that it really is God's fault, that if He cared more "it wouldn't be so bad"? Have you ever thought that perhaps God really is just too busy for you? I know that in my own life, even in the midst of walking with Jesus, I have come to the conclusion that God is letting me down, that He does not truly have my best interest in mind. Sound familiar? Adam and Eve's legacy continues on thousands of years later... thanks guys. Especially in American culture (but I'm no anthropologist) we believe that God wants good things for us. We believe that He wants to make us prosperous! I mean, doesn't the Bible say that? Only someone who is loving, kind and good, could act that way, so if "non-good" things happen, what does that then say about God? This is where the rubber meets the road, and our box is revealed. This is where God uses the disconnect to challenge us toward thinking out of the box.

God Needs Me

There's a myth that we either consciously or subconsciously buy into. Somehow and somewhere along the road of life, we began to believe that God only has a limited amount of caring. I mean this in the broad, general sense of God's goodwill toward Mankind. Therefore, when we are let down, it can shake our perspective. Our natural reaction then is to declare God's need for our part in the Holy Quadrant because He's slipping up (settle down, I'm making a point, not committing blasphemy). This makes sense if we think about the parents, relatives, friends, teachers, or others who we thought we could trust, but have let us down. How about that time your spouse did something that reminded you of your ex? Or, your boss triggers you because one time at your last job you were run over. Be honest, you're telling me you have never grabbed something from your kid only to do it for them because you could do it better and faster? In most cases, we end up trying to control for self-protection and preservation. It makes sense right? For example, if I do not feel safe, then I need to figure out how to feel safe, so I then figure out how to better predict the circumstances around me.

Whether we like it or not, how we interact in the "human" world influences how we interact with God.

KEN SYLVIA

Whether we like it or not, how we interact in the "human" world influences how we interact with God. In fact, research has shown in a variety of contexts that how we interact with our earthly father will translate to how we interact with our Heavenly Father. Without even knowing we are doing it, we will put God in that box, grab the reins of control, and march on. As I am writing this book, God revealed to me that if people I care about are not improving in a time frame or manner that I expect them to, I have a pattern of brushing them aside or becoming critical of who they are. So, how do you think I see God at times? You got it... "Dear God, you're not doing what I want or ask for in my timeframe, so I'll just go ahead and take care of that for you." And in the great words of Maui, "You're welcome!"

Humility and Submission

Breaking out of this pattern requires a very specific mental posture. Like working out, we must exercise it strategically and consistently. It can be challenging (and terrifying) to reflect on our motives, reasoning, and behavior, but self-reflection is the key to opening that box that we have put God in. By searching for what is within us, we allow God to speak into those uncomfortable places. After all, He knows us better than we know ourselves (Romans 8).

This searching within demands a posture of humility and submission. We must be willing to analyze the parts of our souls where we have concluded God is not big enough, and instead elevated ourselves as false gods. Rather than shoving God into the box that we think He fits in, we must build a discipline of honestly approaching that box, and inviting God to step out revealing something new about Himself.

The book of Psalms is filled with examples of David crying out to God. His anger, fear, sadness, pain, hope, faith, and every emotion you can think of vividly comes out directed toward God. David understood that God was way bigger than any box he could dream of, and disciplined a heart after God. Regarding this predicament of humility and submission, I think of David's declaration in Psalms 121:1, "Where does my help come from? My help comes from the Lord, the Maker of Heaven and Earth." As we crack open that box, let us model that mental posture of David, and be assured that God is right here ready to help, engaged in the process, understanding of our weaknesses, and patient as we wrestle.

Adjusting Expectation

God is big, He's just not big enough. God can heal the deadliest of illness, but He can't change my spouse's heart. God can raise the dead to life, but good luck with my parent's attitude. God can impregnate a young teenage girl to carry God in flesh via the Holy Spirit, but He seems nowhere to be found in the middle of my crisis. God says He won't give me more than I can handle, yet the boat is literally sinking, and I'm not the best swimmer. These are all great, but painful examples of God trying to expand our expectation of Him.

Let's revisit the meeting with my mentor at breakfast as I described in the Introduction to this book. As I sat there venting about my frustrations and struggles with my wife, he helped me to discover that my problem in all of that was me! It was *my* problem that *she* wasn't doing what *I* wanted in a way that *I* expected. Instead of going to God through prayer and fasting, and asking Him to help me support my wife in her spiritual growth and her walk with the Lord, I was trying to fix and change her so she'd be on *my* page, to satisfy *my* expectations... for *my* benefit. I didn't trust God to be big enough to develop my wife and help her to grow in her relationship with Him. Not only was I getting in the way of our relationship, I was getting in the way of God doing His work in her life.

We have to be humble and submissive enough to God's sovereignty in order to see a bigger picture. Jeremiah 29:11 is a popular verse that says, "'For I know the plans I have for you,'" declares the Lord, "'plans to prosper you and not to harm you, plans to give you hope and a future.'" For those of you reading who are unaware of this verse's context, it was written to the Israelite nation *after* they were carried away into exile in Babylon.

Imagine one morning you wake up to make some eggs over easy, a slice of toast, maybe even some crispy bacon, and start that first cup of coffee. Life is good! You've got your robe and slippers on, the dawn is breaking through, and you pull back the blinds. God's brilliance radiates and you soak it in. Light beams in, and you feel that warm glow of the morning. After preparing your plate, you step outside as the steam rises from your mug. You scroll through your Bible app, thanking God for His goodness, taking in a deep breath for this new day.

Seemingly out of nowhere flaming arrows strike through your windows, screams, and shouts fill your neighborhood, uproar is everywhere, people are running, falling over themselves, flames consume nearby houses, and before you know it, you are being drug off. Not only did you not finish breakfast (incredibly tragic), but you're defenseless, helpless, half-naked, and beaten with shame. Just like that, in the blink of an eye, your entire world was flipped upside down, even though this morning's devotional was about God's blessings in our lives.

As your feet scrape against the dirty concrete, being led off in chains, the local preacher smiles and awkwardly waves a couple fingers as his hands are tightly bound, exclaiming, "Don't worry, God has a plan for your future." Well, this is what happened to the Israelites. God allowed this nation to go through a period of captivity as a way to prune them and remind them that He is the true and living God and that He is definitely big enough.

The pain and abuse of captivity were a part of God's plans for the people that He loved because He saw a bigger picture. This is an extreme example, but the point is that when things do not go according to our plans or methods, we want to begin exercising command over the situation, "God step aside, I'll take it from here!" God sees the end game in our temporary, long-term, and eternal lives, but all we can see is the right here, right now and use history and past experiences to guide the beliefs and decisions of the here and now.

It is difficult to trust that God really is as big and powerful as He says He is. It is even more difficult, to trust that God has a plan in mind that is even bigger and better than what we can see directly in front of us. If we learn anything from the Israelites, it is that oftentimes God allows incredible challenges and pain so that we have the potential for something greater on the other side. We have to be willing to ride the wave, stick to the journey, and pray for wisdom along the way. Attempting to take control may very well be the thing that keeps us from reaching the other side. However, I acknowledge that it can very well feel like a sick, twisted game, but embracing the pain and discomfort of letting God expand (or even blow up) our box is the very thing we need to mature.

Reflect on the examples of Ezekiel, Samuel, Isaiah, and Jeremiah. These prophets had tough jobs often delivering bad news to bad kings with bad attitudes. Yet each of them maintained a - mostly - healthy trust in God's plan, purpose, and power. They believed God was big enough and so they stayed the course, they didn't sway from the mission at hand. In fact, Isaiah tells us from his story in Isaiah 8:

"The Lord has given me a strong warning not to think like everyone else does. He said, 'Don't call everything a conspiracy, like they do, and don't live in dread of what frightens them. Make the Lord of Heaven's Armies holy in your life. He is the one you should fear. He is the one who should make you tremble...' I will wait for the Lord, who has turned away from the descendants of Jacob. I will put my hope in him."

In the midst of chaos, rebellion, and judgment, Isaiah stays connected to the Source. He is filled with security in the One whose name is "I AM". Isaiah could have easily figured out a way to manipulate those in power, use fancy words to impress, or implement a carefully constructed business plan for the nation of Israel, but instead, he turns to God and declares His greatness. I admit to you that this is something I am not very good at, so I write this book not out of authority, but out of humility understanding that even though I believe some things to be cognitively true about God, I struggle emotionally to grasp onto those truths.

It is true that Isaiah's situation was probably more intense than what we are familiar with, yet there is a quiet truth in his attitude. *God is big enough*! He is big enough for the little things that we think we "can just take care of", and the big things that seem impossible. When we come to the place where we find our peace and rest in knowing that God is truly larger, stronger, wiser, and greater than we will ever be, *then* we will be able to approach our relationships with God and people with a whole new perspective!

STICK & CARROT...
OR MAYBE A COOKIE

CHAPTER 3

LIE #2: GOD IS JUST PLAYING WITH ME.

The Stick & Carrot... Or Maybe a Cookie

Lie #2: God is just playing with me

Have you ever felt like you're running on a treadmill and God is your personal trainer with a big stick and a carrot? You just keep running and striving, but it feels like no matter how hard you push, it is never enough. Right as you think you might have gotten there God pulls up on the stick, you fly into the wall, and He falls over laughing at you. Personally, I am not a big fan of carrots and have no desire to run after them, but if you want to use the analogy of a freshly baked, gooey chocolate chip cookie, then you and I definitely have this in common.

Many times, I have wondered if God really had my best interest in mind. I have wondered if the pain was worth it, or if it was just God wanting to get a good rise out of me. Besides salivating over the thought of milk and cookies, I can't help but wonder how many of us operate our lives on the premise that God is some evil personal trainer who gets more pleasure from watching us aimlessly run than progressing somehow. I am not suggesting God is evil, but that in spite of cognitive affirmation that God really does want to do good things for us, our hearts scream in agony like a guinea pig on one of those silly spinning wheels that never stops.

Somewhere along the line, we bought into the lie that God is playing this game that requires a certain level of performance, and if we fail to meet the requirements we get flung from the treadmill (or spinning wheel) while He watches and laughs. Maybe this belief (or attitude) toward God stems from parental upbringing or traumatic life experiences, or maybe it comes from a broken dream that you were certain would come true. I think of the movie *Tron* that was released a few years ago. It can sometimes feel like the program called "Life" is specifically designed to always give us the disadvantage, and the only way to be victorious is to "think outside the box". We redefine how life *should* work so that we can protect ourselves from unnecessary hurts. We end up wrestling with God because, as Adam and Eve thought, He is holding out on us, He is teasing us, or perhaps He is waiting for that last second to pull up on the stick.

I don't think anyone really believes that God has based His entire existence on the opportunity to mess with us, but when the moment success or peace settles in, we start looking over our shoulders for something terrible to happen. In fact, I met with a young man I was mentoring not too long ago who told me, "Where I come from, I have to look over my shoulder because I never know who is out for me next." This broke my heart and made me wonder how many more people are out there who have this same knee-jerk-reaction. How many people out there have a compulsory twitch of the head to look over each shoulder to ensure survival? And, how many of them view God as unable to be fully trusted because of this experience? I'm not sure I can relate in exactly the same way, but I would be lying to you if I said I never had that knot in my stomach the moment after something good happened waiting for something bad to strike. Sometimes it seems like with each blessing that we receive, it makes the following drop of disappointment that much more painful.

I never really witnessed a healthy marriage growing up. I love my parents and I know full well that they feel guilty over how things worked out, yet because of their brokenness, there were definitely times when I felt like the pawn in their chess game. Holidays were rarely fun because it typically meant there was going to be a fight over who's turn it was to have me, even though I knew it was because they both wanted time with me, and to be around their side of the family. Needless to say, the idea of getting married was a difficult and painful concept for me to consider as my wife and I grew closer and closer together. In fact, we now joke about how she used to say, "You want to be with me forever-*ever?*" and I would mumble, "Um, maybe just forever. Forever-ever feels a little extreme"

The Voice in the Room

My wife and I had a very rocky dating relationship, and we can now look back and say that it was completely God in the midst of the storm because no matter how difficult the relationship was, or what issues we were facing, we felt drawn together more and more through prayer, fasting and seeking the Lord. One night, as I was alone in my house I began just talking to God, as if He was physically in the room. You have to understand that this was a two-story house with a basement and it was completely dark inside. Only the streetlights and car lights shined through. I was just having one of those days where I was "freaking out" about the idea of marriage and whether or not my wife was really the "right person" for me. I began talking to Him, which turned into a plea for help, which became a cry in confusion and fear and was only interrupted by silent groans in pain. As the "conversation" continued on, which was really me having an angry, yelling episode, I became so amped up and angry at Him for all of this pain, I stopped to yell out, "What the $%&# are you doing?! What do you want from me?!"

Now you have to understand that this was a pivotal night for me. This was significant, not only to facing my fears with my wife, but also in my relationship with my Creator, Father, and Friend. I can remember the weather, where I was at, the layout of the room, the smells in the air, and the entire episode as if it had been saved in the "Moments to Remember" folder on my hard drive.

So here I am yelling and cursing and pacing like an upset tiger in a cage, when I once more exclaimed,

"What is your problem?!" and God said, as clear as a THX-certified theater, "Now, stop right there, you've crossed a line. Why do you think that my only goal in life is to hurt you?" I remember, as if it were yesterday, stopping in my tracks, falling to the floor, and weeping. My response was, "God, I keep waiting for you to pull up on the stick, watch me fall over the cliff, and then peer over it laughing at me, chuckling, 'Ha! I gotcha!'" Then, as tender as a Loving Perfect Father could, said to me, "Son, I died on the cross for you, do you really think I would go through all of that only to play tricks with you?"

I wrestled with God that night, and He became real to me in an entirely new dimension. I had struggled, manipulated, controlled, seized, grasped, and attempted to exercise command over a "stick" that wasn't even there. I thought that I was in this game of chess, trying to outmaneuver God so that I could grab the stick and claim the prize. However, as I reflected on this night, I realized I had a lot more in common with the great patriarch Jacob as he too wrestled with God.

Jacob's Struggle and Desire to be Blessed

The first half of Genesis 32 tells the story of Jacob's brother, Esau, hunting him down because he had manipulated and tricked him into stealing their father's blessings. Jacob sent out messengers to try and woo him, but the response back was that he didn't exactly look happy and had four hundred men with him ready to slaughter everyone. Jacob then comes up with a scheme to divide the party in half so that at least some could be saved, and then pleads with God to spare his life, even making sure to throw a couple prayers up to remind God that he had promised his ancestor Abraham that his descendants would be greater than the sand on the seashore, "so nothing better happen to me, because You said so, and if I'm not around you can't keep your promise to Grandpa Abe." Finally, just in case, Jacob adds a cherry on top by sending waves of gifts hoping to appease his brother.

Though one would logically argue that it was only rational to try and do everything humanly possible to calm down a very well prepared and determined hunter, the truth of the matter is that Jacob was exercising command in every way possible to control the situation. I'm not arguing as to whether this made sense or not, but simply making the point that it *seems* his intent and motivation was to exercise command over the situation, because other than throwing up a couple "just in case" prayers to God, that was not his primary strategy. Ultimately, Genesis 32 would have been written much differently had Esau never sold his birthright. Nonetheless, Jacob schemed and manipulated his way into the situation to get the blessing from his father.

The most interesting thing happens between the point of showering his brother with bribes and then meeting him the following day in Genesis 33. Jacob wrestles with God. Genesis 32:22-31 tells the story:

> *22 That night Jacob got up and took his two wives, his two maidservants and his eleven sons and crossed the ford of the Jabbok. 23 After he had sent them across the stream,*

he sent over all his possessions. **24** *So Jacob was left alone,*
and a man wrestled with him till daybreak. **25** *When the*
man saw that he could not overpower him, he touched the
socket of Jacob's hip so that his hip was wrenched as he
wrestled with the man. **26** *Then the man said, "Let me go,*
for it is daybreak." But Jacob replied, "I will not let you go
unless you bless me." **27** *The man asked him, "What is*
your name?" "Jacob," he answered. **28** *Then the man said,*
"Your name will no longer be Jacob, but Israel, because you
have struggled with God and with men and have overcome."
29 *Jacob said, "Please tell me your name." But he replied,*
"Why do you ask my name?" Then he blessed him there.
30 *So Jacob called the place Peniel, saying, "It is because I*
saw God face to face, and yet my life was spared." **31** *The*
sun rose above him as he passed Peniel, and he was limping
because of his hip.

Jacob was willing to become physically injured over his
deep desire and hunger for a blessing. He not only stole
what was rightfully his brother's but then wrestled God
in human form – I don't want to even try and figure that
out – and won with the "blessing" as the prize.

Maybe you haven't literally, or even figuratively wrestled
with God, but doesn't it make sense that our deepest
desire is to know that God wants to bless us? Don't
we all want assurance that despite the chaos, craziness,
and coldness of life, that the Creator of everything is
inherently loving, kind, compassionate, good, and just?
Don't we want to experience the greatness, goodness, and
power of the Almighty in our lives?

This "blessing" that we seek from God is not about material things, though He may choose to allow such measures. No, God's definition of blessing is something very different. God's definition of blessing – in my humble opinion – is the mental, emotional and spiritual connection to the goodness, greatness, and power of God-Almighty. We are blessed when He empowers us to love Him with all of our heart, soul, mind, and strength on a deeper level than we could before. After wrestling with God, Jacob became Israel. He was not only physically changed, but he was also spiritually changed. The schemer became a founder. The liar became a champion. The scoundrel became a hero. Wrestling with the Almighty revealed that his idea of a blessing had been skewed and that what he really wanted could only be given by God.

Similarly, I did not begin seeking God that night in my house out of a desire to experience His greatness. I sought God out that night for an answer about the pain and confusion I felt about my wife, only to discover that God allowed all of that so I could experience the blessing of hearing His voice in the room echoing that His love for me is measured in the cross. A symbol that no matter how high or deep, and from east to west, nothing could separate me from His love. My heart, my mind, and my soul were changed that night all because I was worried about whether or not I should say, "I do."

I was operating on a definition that a blessing had to be earned, worked for, suffered for and that the blessing was always contingent upon God's current mood. If you have been paying attention, you can probably guess that this is how I experienced a "blessing" growing up. I had to do enough or be good enough. This childhood belief carried over into my adulthood, and God graciously allowed this pain to prune me of a belief that was keeping Him in my box. It has taken me years to come to the place of understanding that it is by His grace, His love, and His forgiveness that I am blessed.

We each have our own unique combination of development, experience, context, upbringing, personality, and the like, and our brains attempt to assemble all of that into a nice, clean, beautiful box that contains God. I had assembled a box that subconsciously qualified my greatness by how driven and excellent I had become. I unknowingly reasoned that God was good in my life because I was so good in my life. However, God's grace was enough and allowed brokenness to turn me to Him. That broken moment in my life was not the actual lesson, but the vehicle to help me see a bigger picture.

The Most Difficult, Problematic Challenge Ever

It does not take an astrophysicist or even a seasoned theologian to explain that problems arise when we project unreal or selfish expectations onto God. When we attempt to exercise command and insert our desires, or will, into God's plans and purposes we find that not only do we disrupt His process, but we can also create relational tension between Him and us.

When we attempt to exercise command and insert our desires, or will, into God's plans and purposes we find that not only do we disrupt His process, but we can also create relational tension between Him and us.

KEN SYLVIA

Many of the latest leadership books written in the last few years talk about the importance of trust. Why is it that we do not, cannot, or will not choose to apply those same principles to our relationship and journey with God?

Trust is so difficult for us because we come from a broken world that celebrates the "self". How can I really trust God when the only thing to compare Him to are self-absorbed humans obsessed with self-promotion, self-improvement, and selfies. If you've been around a teenager for more than one second, they are obsessed with taking pictures of themselves. The world in which we live worships the "self", for good and for bad. In fact, if you take enough pictures of yourself and post them on social media, they will dub you an "influencer"! However, this is not how Jesus led or connected with others.

This isn't a revolutionary concept, selfishness and self-seeking behaviors are rampant throughout the world, in all cultures, and in all people. Jesus was followed because His entire Being was the antithesis of selfishness. Lost, broken people went out of their way to soak up His presence because He saw them, valued them, and blessed them. For once, there was someone who said, "I see you!" rather than "You see me!" Jesus Christ's entire purpose in life was to be in relationship with the Father, thereby glorifying Him in everything He was and in everything He did. Jesus's agenda was relationship and obedience to God the Father, whereas the agenda of the religious leaders, pop stars, and celebrities of the day was: "Me." Look at me! See how I can pray! Make sure you tithe on the way out... for me! Jesus was a stark contrast to these me-seekers to show the world, they do not reflect the *true* God!

Jesus says that there is no greater love than for a friend to lay down his life for another (John 15:13). He tells us that if we are tired from performing, then he offers a sweet vacation spot for the soul at an all-inclusive resort. Jesus says that His burden is light, so there's no need to worry about whether or not we're good enough for Him (Matthew 11:30). And God says, "Hey, you can trust Me. I was so serious about blessing you, I sent my only Son – my Perfect, Spotless Lamb – to die so that there would be no hindrance in our relationship. Why don't you come rest in My Presence, and I'll show you how much I love you." (John 3:16-17)

The most difficult, problematic challenge ever is to rest in His presence. The challenge to say, "God, I will trust you enough to choose to believe that this treadmill I am on right now is actually a forced construct I have placed on You, and actually what you want of me is to step off of that, and just sit down in this soothing lounge chair next to You." Perhaps the most problematic challenge for you is to say, "God, I will choose to trust that You desire to bless me regardless of my performance, regardless of my greatness, because who You are is the Blesser." It is easy to cognitively repeat these things, but it is terrifying to let go of the things that have allowed us to feel comfortable and have kept God in the box.

Transformation comes when we allow God out of that box, crack open our hearts and confess to God what we are really thinking and feeling.

KEN SYLVIA

Transformation comes when we allow God out of that box, crack open our hearts and confess to God what we are really thinking and feeling. Rest in His presence right now. Invite Him to step out of the box and reveal something bigger and better to you.

NO, THIS IS
HOW IT WORKS

CHAPTER 4

LIE #3: CONTROL IS OUR FRIEND.

No, This is how it Works

Lie #3: Control is our friend

The human desire to take control of, or exercise command over a situation, is an attempt at protecting, preserving, or satisfying one's "self". When things become uncomfortable, it is natural to try to exercise command and play the ship captain of Life. This is especially true in relationships because each individual has his or her own sets of stuff. It is one thing to be concerned about work, sports, health, or whatever, but these are the things that we can typically easily fix by setting job expectations, watching what we eat, working out routinely, or yelling at the players on the screen (kidding). However, humans have free will - at least to a certain extent - and so it is not as simple as pressing a button or pumping some iron in order to get your spouse, child, coworker, or house pet to do as you like. Lord knows, my wife and I think we are dog owners, but the truth is that our dog is a human owner.

As finite beings, we can only control what *we* think and how *we* act. Even when we feel someone is "forcing" us to do something, we still usually have an option to do otherwise. This doesn't mean there may not be consequences, but as a rule of thumb, only *you* can control *you*, and only *I* can control *me*. Let's look at an example from one of Peter's less-than-finer moments:

> **21** *From that time on Jesus began to explain to his disciples that he must go to Jerusalem and suffer many things at the hands of the elders, chief priests and teachers of the law, and that he must be killed and on the third day be raised to life.* **22** *Peter took him aside and began to rebuke him. "Never, Lord!" he said. "This shall never happen to you!"* **23** *Jesus turned and said to Peter, "Get behind me, Satan! You are a stumbling block to me; you do not have in mind the things of God, but the things of men."* **24** *Then Jesus said to his disciples, "If anyone would come after me, he must deny himself and take up his cross and follow me.* **25** *For whoever wants to save his life will lose it, but whoever loses his life for me will find it.* **26** *What good will it be for a man if he gains the whole world, yet forfeits his soul? Or what can a man give in exchange for his soul?* **27** *For the Son of Man is going to come in his Father's glory with his angels, and then he will reward each person according to what he has done.* **28** *I tell you the truth, some who are standing here will not taste death before they see the Son of Man coming in his kingdom."*

Mark shares a similar story as in the Matthew 16 passage above, but adds that Jesus "spoke plainly" about His death and resurrection as if it was a matter of fact (see Mark 8:32). Jesus spoke with clarity, certainty, and confidence that it was only a matter of time before He was handed over to the religious leaders to be executed.

Mark 8:34-35 also parallels Matthew 16:24, but adds that there was a "crowd... along with his disciples". Jesus was making sure that all who could hear (including you and me) would know this was one of the most vital elements of a deeper, truer calling.

Jesus throws a huge monkey wrench into the people's hopes and dreams. Up until this point in time, the twelve disciples and the other followers had this idea that Jesus was going to bring down all of Heaven's Armies and wipe out the pesky Romans. They had an unshakeable faith that Jesus was the Messiah, and that His mission was to save His people. In fact, it wasn't long before this episode (see Matthew 16:16) that Peter blurts out in his typical dramatic fashion before all creation that Jesus was and is the "Christ, the Son of the living God." Nobody doubted *who* Jesus was because His words and actions made it clear He was something else. However, the box they had put Jesus into did not allow for Him to accomplish His mission in an unorthodox manner.

God seems to have such a habit of accomplishing His plans and will in a way that is beyond our logical comprehension. This is where control becomes our enemy because it places the conductor's wand into our hands. Practicing submission before the Lord allows Him to not only accomplish great things but to accomplish great things where it is obvious that He is the true conductor. Unfortunately, if we are to truly connect with The Creator in a deeper manner, we must act as He did in the Garden, full of volition, but emptied of self. Perhaps the only way to truly experience God in a grandiose way is to open up that box, crying out, sweating blood, and surrendering that conductor's wand... "Not our will, but Yours be done."

The Argument

When Peter stepped in and began informing Jesus that this whole "dying thing" was nonsense, he was essentially saying, "No Jesus, this is not how it is supposed to work. Your business strategy and overall life plan are all wrong! We cannot conquer the world if you are dead." Up until this point in history, there was no framework in which victory was possible through death. It was a foreign concept. Furthermore, Peter bought into the lie that experiencing pain is bad, whether it is physical, emotional, spiritual, or relational. Not only were Peter's dreams crushed, but he would be losing a close friend. So, it would make perfect sense then that he would try to control the situation by putting Jesus in His place. Peter concluded in his mind that Jesus's scenario could not be beneficial for anyone.

If we are brutally honest with ourselves, we fully grasp that lie. In fact, in America (again, not an anthropologist) we avoid pain like the Plague (or COVID-19), which is technically a good thing, but you know what I mean. We believe pain is bad, therefore we will go to great lengths to control and minimize this pain so that we may experience the mirage of safety and security in the world around us... or in us. In this way, we rationalize that control is actually our friend, there to help guide and protect when discomfort rears its ugly head. However, what we cannot understand is that the very best possible outcome most likely requires some pain, but we have to embrace it.

Let's stop for a moment and imagine Jesus saving the world through some other means. Consider He snaps His fingers with the Infinity Gauntlet, calls upon the 7 Plagues, or summons the sci-fi stuff in Revelation. If I am honest, that's probably a way more entertaining television series, but is that the kind of person you want to surrender your life to? Mary Magdalene, a woman whose reputation wasn't that of the girl you would want your son to date, was the first person to see Jesus after the resurrection. Someone who was considered unclean sought after and was welcomed in by God in flesh. Jesus was a leader who laid down His own life for those He loved and attracted those who the rich and famous had cast aside. This is not how I would have written the story if I was in control (thank God)!

Surrender is the posture
by which God works miracles
in us and through us.

KEN SYLVIA

Surrender is the posture by which God works miracles in us and through us. For most of us, it requires opening up that box and redefining how we see Him. This posture has the power to elicit empathy which is to connect on a deeper level with another's situation. It communicates that we acknowledge we are not actually in control but are in need of the One who is. Surrender is a posture that invites others to help. It encourages community to come together, especially when we process the difficult moments in our lives.

We all have wounds. Some may have more wounds or deeper wounds, but the reality is that life hurts, and it leaves us with what my counselor calls an "emotional bookmark". These wounds affect how we see ourselves, others, and God, and how we relate to each. It is vital that we first be open and honest about these wounds because secrecy and darkness are where Evil loves to hide. We must also take the necessary steps to find healing whether through professional counseling, mentors, or God's Word. Vulnerability opens us up to the potential of being hurt, but it also opens us up to the potential of experiencing deep healing. Trustworthy community connections can play a major role in living a life that God has called us to. God can use our pain for His purposes if we choose to surrender.

Peter also had a serious relational dilemma. He was one of Jesus' closest friends, and he was not interested in hearing about his friend's brutal murder. Peter was saddened, hurt, and most likely afraid when he considered the inevitability of Jesus's death, but I would also bet that Peter was concerned with how Jesus's death would personally affect him. We are relational beings and we make choices based on relational consequences, both good and bad. Peter was operating on those relational concerns and stepped in to intervene in order to minimize any damage. He needed Jesus to stay in the box that he had created because trying to open that up left Peter vulnerable.

From a humanistic perspective, Peter's reaction is a normal one. I haven't conducted thorough research, but I think it is safe to assume that 99.9999% of all people would try to talk their B.F.F. (best friend forever in case you were wondering) out of voluntarily being murdered. It is against all human intuition and basic survival skills to go through something as painful as a death on a cross. Perhaps even more so when such undeserved pain is willingly volunteered for. God in the form of the Son of Man saw the bigger picture and knew that the sacrifice of a spotless lamb was required for freedom and salvation to be possible.

The Response

In the Matthew 16 passage, Jesus immediately reacts to Peter, "Get behind me Satan!" Jesus stops Peter mid-step and cuts him off from his logical plea to not follow through with certain death. That passage also says that Peter "began to rebuke" Jesus, insinuating that Peter didn't actually get all the way through his intended monologue. Like that night in the house when Jesus stopped me mid-meltdown, He reacts in such a way as to remind Peter, the disciples, the crowd, *and Himself* that this was what needed to happen for the sake of the bigger picture. There was no other option and there was no argument that was going to change God's will and plans.

Not only does Jesus call Peter "Satan", but then has the boldness, in front of the "crowd" nonetheless, to exclaim that Peter was being selfishly shortsighted. Jesus clarifies that those only worthy enough to be considered His followers must deny themselves and pick up their crosses and follow Him. Now, you have to remember that in this culture, the cross was a symbol and method of capital punishment reserved for the worst of criminals. Jesus was trying to convey that to be a true follower of the Messiah, self-denial is central to discipleship. Furthermore, true followers of the Way had to be willing to obey the will and plans of the Father, disregarding the "self's" interest.

For Peter and all the others around listening to this conversation, self-denial meant throwing away the idea that the Messiah was going to be this amazing hero with fiery swords, an infinite supply of armor-piercing arrows, and the voice of Mel Gibson in *Braveheart*. Jesus says in John 10:15 that it is by His own volition that *He* lays down *His* life for the sheep. The heroism of the Messiah was not found in battle-ready attire, rather self-denial, loneliness, and anguish. Peter had to get it through his thick skull that Jesus was born to die so that we might have life everlasting. Jesus' mission was to come as a servant and lay down His life for the living, the dead, and the yet to be born. This was a concept – a way of believing – that radically shook Peter, the disciples, and the "crowd".

His followers had to let go of their preconceived ideas about who Jesus was and how He was going to be victorious. Allowing God to work in *His* way requires that we loosen our imaginative grip on whatever it is that we are holding on to. Of course, this is an absolutely terrifying concept because it comes with the feeling that we are losing (or have lost) all control. But, the truth is that by letting go of a box that does not contain Jesus, or at least an accurate version of Him, allows us to gain a more intimate experience with Him.

Learning to let go requires learning how to trust.

KEN SYLVIA

Learning to let go requires learning how to trust. We have to know that what we are about to lean into will stay steadfast. Sometimes it is easy to reflect on the first-hand experiences where God has shown Himself to be trustworthy, while other times we have to just throw our hands in the air knowing that there really is no other option other than taking that first step of faith. Jesus reminds Peter, and us, in the Matthew 16 interaction that He has proven Himself over and over again that even when things do not make perfect sense to us, He knows what He is doing.

The night that I had a meltdown in the Lord's presence was not the night that I "let go" of all the "what ifs" in regard to the relationship with my wife, it was the night I began interacting with my Savior on the foundation that He was big enough for me. I realized that it didn't matter what all the "what ifs" could be because gaining all the ulcers in the world would not prevent any of that from happening anyway. I came to terms with the fact that unless I wanted to go live isolated in a monastery, I was going to have people issues. Even though I could not physically see God that night, I knew it was Him entering my world, speaking to me, and showing me something I was not capable of seeing prior. Even though we cannot see, we know that there is still evidence surrounding us proving His hands are stretched out toward us.

What if God Calls us to Pain?

I love the book *Anonymous* by Alicia Britt Chole because she does an excellent job making Jesus' "hidden years" come alive. She illuminates the parts of the story that are so often overlooked. In a world that celebrates noise, glamour, and the façade, it is uncommon to find those that reflect on those more hidden moments, and openly share how they have been impacted because of them. Obviously, I am making a vast generalization, but let's stop to consider the people in our immediate circles of influence. Do you really know their whole story? Are they vulnerable with their moments of fear and shame? Are you cracking open your heart and exposing the things inside that could leave others with a different opinion if they really knew what you were thinking and feeling? To some, the idea of doing such a thing makes their pulse speed up and sweat drip off their forehead. Control has been their friend for so long that keeping their soul in the dark sounds better than the possibility of experiencing something great.

I confess that I have always been an open individual. Perhaps one of my bigger flaws is that I say more than I should at times. However, I am calculated with what I share. While I am honest, I rarely put myself in a vulnerable position. I share what I share if I think that sharing what I share can help my cause in some way. You follow? I have shared pieces of my story to thousands of junior high and high school students, yet few people really know those deeper things that haunt me. Why? Because I don't want to be rejected! Yet, when I have shared those moments of vulnerability, I find that generally, people connect with me because they too have experienced something similar. I will never forget one time I shared about a particularly painful experience at a local high school and at the end of the session during group time, a young man stands up and confesses to the whole room a struggle he had. Then says to me, "Because of your story, I feel like I can talk about what I've been dealing with on the inside." Appropriately sharing a painful experience empowered this young man to open up, and while I will never know the exponential impact of such an act, I allowed my story to be used for His glory.

Accepting the pain in our lives and processing through those experiences will draw us and those around us with whom we share our stories closer to God. As much as it hurts, we must resist acting like Peter and doing whatever it takes to avoid the pain. Instead, we must surrender, and acknowledge that only He can get us through it, and only He can use it for something beautiful that we cannot yet see. I would argue that this is true discipleship. Peter had to look himself in the metaphorical mirror and ask whether or not he was really willing to follow Jesus, even if it meant losing Him.

Discipleship demands pain and loss. Following someone else requires modification of our behavior to more align with the one we are following. In this case, Jesus gave up His life. Therefore, we must give ourselves up if we are to truly know God in an intimate way. Jesus asks us to pick up our cross, and follow Him. Imagine Jesus advertises the following on a billboard: "Follow me! You'll be challenged, you'll suffer, and at times you'll wonder if it's really worth it!" Right below the billboard, an aluminum green sign with reflective white letters lists the upcoming towns:

- Painville   5 miles
- Rejectedton   25 miles
- San Follower   200 miles

Jesus is not cruel or waiting to jerk us around as we covered in the previous chapter. No, He informs us ahead of time that the destination is not going to be easy. If we are going to follow, we must learn to trust that God really is big enough. He is big enough in our pain. He is big enough in our weakness. He is big enough to use anything we go through for a more beautiful ending.

ONE SMALL STEP

CHAPTER 5

LIE #4: IT WILL ALL FALL APART.

One Small Step...

Lie #4: It will all fall apart

"Sometimes letting things go is an act of far greater power than defending or hanging on." ~ *Eckhart Tolle*

"The man who moves a mountain begins by carrying away small stones." ~ *Confucius*

"Faith… is the art of holding on to things your reason has once accepted, in spite of your changing moods." ~ *C.S. Lewis*

I like the scene in *Indiana Jones- Last Crusade* where Harrison Ford, playing Dr. Jones, must step out onto this invisible bridge as an act of faith in order to cross the deathly chasm. Perhaps I am oversimplifying this concept, but this analogy of taking one small step at a time into an invisible territory is what must happen in order to begin prying our metaphorical fingers off "Command Central". Likewise, opening a box can be really exciting if you trust who it's from. Or, it can require the bomb squad. Either way, you must have the faith to open one flap at a time.

Faith is taking steps toward something that is not clearly seen, and trusting that walking in that direction will not result in the entire world crumbling beneath us. How many of us have felt terrified to make a decision? How many of us have been crippled by the thought of the unknown? Yet, isn't that a daily reality? Nonetheless, we weigh the odds and make decisions. We take our belief systems and carry them over our shoulder out into the world to manipulate as much as we can, or at least one at a time.

If we really think about it, we have little to absolutely no control over what happens in life around us. Yes, we can control what we choose to do in any given moment, but there is very little we can do to control the outcomes of the external world around us. From the decisions our friends and family make to whether we will all have jobs tomorrow morning, we live in a daily reality of the uncomfortable unknown. We are at the mercy of selfishness, brokenness, fragility, and the never-ending news cycle.

Whether we are aware of it or not, or whether we'd like to acknowledge it or not, we are all asking the same question: "What will happen if...?" This is the million-dollar question. If we had the supernatural ability to see beyond the immediate consequences of our actions and of those around us, it would drastically impact how we live our lives. In fact, if there was some way we could harness God's omniscient and omnipresent powers, and program them into a simple algorithm we would be billionaires! Imagine, for five easy payments of $29.99 you could own *What Will Happen Tomorrow* and never have to worry, fear, or sweat ever again! Act now, and you can have the free *Change Others Around You Tool*, just pay shipping and handling!

As I read and study God's Word more and more, I have come to the realization that the entire Bible is about proving God is big enough for us. He is sufficient and He perfectly satisfies every need and want we can truly have. So, He has provided hundreds of stories of people who struggled with truly believing this principle. From Adam and Eve, to Abraham and Sarah, to David and the census, to... take your pick. As my mentor would say, "God is a big boy, He knows what He is doing."

Learning to let go of our perceived command and learning to trust God in His ultimate and supreme command, in my humble opinion, is the goal of life. My reasoning for this is found in the final moments of Jesus Christ's human existence. Matthew 26: 36-46 tells the story of Jesus struggling with God over His lack of control... which we'll see is His willingness to humble Himself to the Father's will.

> **36** *Then Jesus went with his disciples to a place called Gethsemane, and he said to them, "Sit here while I go over there and pray." **37** He took Peter and the two sons of Zebedee along with him, and he began to be sorrowful and troubled. **38** Then he said to them, "My soul is overwhelmed with sorrow to the point of death. Stay here and keep watch with me." **39** Going a little farther, he fell*

with his face to the ground and prayed, "My Father, if it is possible, may this cup be taken from me. Yet not as I will, but as you will." 40 Then he returned to his disciples and found them sleeping. "Could you men not keep watch with me for one hour?" he asked Peter. 41 "Watch and pray so that you will not fall into temptation. The spirit is willing, but the body is weak." 42 He went away a second time and prayed, "My Father, if it is not possible for this cup to be taken away unless I drink it, may your will be done." 43 When he came back, he again found them sleeping, because their eyes were heavy. 44 So he left them and went away once more and prayed the third time, saying the same thing. 45 Then he returned to the disciples and said to them, "Are you still sleeping and resting? Look, the hour is near, and the Son of Man is betrayed into the hands of sinners. 46 Rise, let us go! Here comes my betrayer!"

I find it interesting that Luke, the good doctor, tells a shortened, yet more detailed story of the same event in Luke 22: 40-46...

39 Jesus went out as usual to the Mount of Olives, and his disciples followed him. 40 On reaching the place, he said to them, "Pray that you will not fall into temptation." 41 He withdrew about a stone's throw beyond them, knelt down and prayed, 42 "Father, if you are willing, take this cup from me; yet not my will, but yours be done." 43 An angel from heaven appeared to him and strengthened him. 44 And being in anguish, he prayed more earnestly, and his sweat was like drops of blood falling to the ground. 45 When he rose from prayer and went back to the disciples, he found them asleep, exhausted from sorrow. 46 "Why are you sleeping?" he asked them. "Get up and pray so that you will not fall into temptation."

I do not intend to try and explain the theories behind the details in Luke's story versus that of Matthew. However, I think it is important to note that Luke's story enhances the severe distress and inner turmoil that Jesus was experiencing. He understood that He was the "Son of Man" (God in human flesh). We have to assume that if Jesus has the power to feed thousands from a nice snack, bring the dead back to life, and calm nature's grumpiness, then He also had the power to control this situation. If the same guy who was able to overcome His own death, then surely He could have chosen to exercise command, "Nope, I'm not doing this. Let's put together a committee to look at alternatives." In His infinite wisdom, Jesus had to have been arguing with God about a vast number of options, plans, and compromises. Yet, He chooses to continue seeking the Father's will, begging for any other option.

This story shows that Jesus was not only human, in the pure sense of the word, but He too struggled with letting God maintain control of the situation. Jesus had an angelic, blood-drenched, sleepless night of anguish over something He absolutely did not want to do. And who could blame Him? God knows I could not have done it. Although we see His humanity through this experience, His connection with the Father is bright and clear. An angel comes and strengthens Jesus in His moment of frailty. While the angel's visit does not fix the situation, as Luke records Jesus going right back to anguish and bloody sweat, but that angelic visit seems to move Jesus into the next phase of the journey.

Connected to a Perfect, Loving Father

Jesus had a deep, intimate relationship with the Father, and it was through this bond Jesus had a fool-proof trust of His Father's perfect will that helped Him to persevere and endure this horrific experience. At the end of the night, at about the same time as His betrayer's arrival, He gets up, awakens the disciples, and faces His imminent doom. Jesus had a limitless box (intentional oxymoron) to know that somehow in this crazy scheme, God-Almighty, the Great I AM knew exactly what He was doing and had a perfect plan in place.

If it is true that Jesus Christ is all-knowing, then his God-self knew that He was in fact the sacrificial lamb, and a horrifying death was His Father's "Plan A", and there was no way around that. However, Jesus was fully God *and* fully man (don't know how that worked, but it's on my shortlist of important questions when I get to Heaven), which means his Man-self must have been wondering whether or not his feet would find the invisible bridge once he stepped into the treacherous abyss. He had to have been wondering, "Is it going to be worth it? Will I really recover from this death? Will my death actually cure sin?"

In the midst of a horrible, difficult, and painful situation Jesus chooses to actively stay grounded in His connection to the Father, and in doing so, pushes His own will aside. Doesn't this run counterintuitive to our instincts? Since the first sin of our known world, we have been fighting God over who gets to be in control. Is there a history lesson where this isn't true? We believe that myth – or even the lie – that if I let go of command, then the whole thing is going to fall apart. There's this struggle within us that demands we be in life's driver seat. I have worked with thousands of young people, and the one thing I find common among the vast majority: pride. Everywhere from the teachers and parents being the problem to low self-esteem, the common denominator is that they believe the world revolves around them, and if things in life do not go perfectly, they do not have the perspective or discipline to ask, "God, what are you teaching me here?" Whether it is conscious or not, even we adults believe to some degree that God cannot truly be in control if we are not involved. This causes us to insert our wills into places that are not intended for them.

Do not mistake what I am saying here. We are absolutely commanded to serve the poor, the widows, the jailed, the broken, the helpless, the abused, the forgotten, and the marginalized. But, we are to do this connected to the Father. I would argue that you should not even give a homeless person $1 without first asking God to direct you. I would argue that you should not become involved in some social program, speaking engagement, business opportunity, relationship, or anything else without – at the very minimum – stopping to consider whether this is really God's direction in your life, or you simply acting for your own self-interest. Acting out of self-interest (selfishness) isn't intrinsically bad, but self-interest and God-interest are not always on the same path.

The truth is that God understands our "humanness". The writer of Hebrews reassures us in chapter 4, verse 15 that "we do not have a high priest who is unable to sympathize with our weaknesses, but we have one who has been tempted in every way, just as we are–yet was without sin." Jesus knows what it is like when everything inside of us is screaming to grab the reigns of our lives and situations and take command. Jesus did not *have* to die for us. "What?!" you say. "Heretic!" you exclaim. Stop and think about it... He could have said no. Jesus followed through with God's plan for no reason other than His complete, unwavering trust and obedience to His Father. As we saw in earlier chapters here, He surrendered Himself for the sake of a bigger picture.

A very wise mentor and professor of mine once said that trusting God is like leaving your palms open facing the sky with whatever issue, situation, or circumstance is troubling you. He then said, "True practice of faith means to leave them open seeking God's will in the process. Perhaps God will take it from you and you can close your palms, or perhaps God is asking you to throw whatever concern it is away as if to say, 'God, this is your problem, not mine.' However, the most difficult option is the one where God says... nothing. Your palms are open, you're seeking an answer, begging for direction, and God's response is: 'keep them open'. This is the epitome of faith. The same faith Dr. Jones had when he stepped into the chasm, and the same faith Jesus had when he allowed himself to be betrayed."

The most important part of this analogy is the relationship with the Father. If we are actively seeking

Him, not only as our Wonderful Counselor (Guide) but primarily as our Father and Friend, then surely it will work out... won't it? The issue lies in humbling ourselves, letting go of the reigns, and being willing to submit ourselves to whatever God sees appropriate. As we will discuss in further detail later on, this is all for our benefit, to transform us more-so into the Image of His Son, Jesus Christ.

Living our lives with our spiritual (and perhaps physical) palms wide open is a painful thing to do because it is what leaves us most vulnerable. It can make us feel like we are defenseless, open to more pain, more attack, and much less control. Though these feelings may very well be valid, they operate on the lie that God has that stick out watching us jump for the prize, but continually pulling it up at the last second, chuckling in that deep thunderous voice "Ah haha! Gotcha!"

Biggest Lie Ever

So, I will admit upfront, perhaps it's not the "biggest" lie ever, but I think it ranks among the Top 10: "Let go and Let God". Isn't that catchy? It sounds really cute and fits (way too) well on most bumper stickers. Plus, you can tweet it real fast, and no one can argue against it because it makes them sound unspiritual. Lucky for you, I am trying to be unspiritual for the sake of making a point. So, let's break this saying down and dissect what it is trying to communicate.

The first half is "Let go". Though I think this has good intention, it falls short and is very humanistic – even selfish – in nature. While "letting go" may be a good thing, depending on our situation at hand, it may not be what God is calling us to. Maybe He is calling us to hold on, maybe He is calling us to wrestle or maybe... there are other options that we haven't sought His wisdom and direction on, but you can't fit this sentence on a bumper sticker.

Imagine you are holding a hot plate in your hand. Perhaps you can hold it for a few seconds, but once that burning sensation starts to set in, we immediately seek to rid ourselves of the pain. In this case, letting go is a reaction, not a deliberate, intentional action. On the other hand, no pun intended, imagine you have a very difficult family member who continually lets you down, disappoints and makes destructive decisions that are beyond your control. In this case, doesn't it sound only natural to acknowledge the truth of our inability to control, and "let go" of those feelings or desires? The answer is still no, because it is not as simple as letting go.

The truth here is that when you choose to remove yourself from the position of Chief Control Officer, you are simultaneously, intentionally and deliberately choosing to *take on* the position of Humbled Servant. It is in this position that we recognize the Lordship of Jesus Christ, modeling his behavior, and transforming us into His image.

Though we might relinquish control over our "power", we are actually gaining a higher power that can demonstrate the wonder of God.

KEN SYLVIA

Though we might relinquish control over our "power", we are actually gaining a higher power that can demonstrate the wonder of God.

The second half of that saying says, "...let God". Maybe I'm just being nit-picky, but have you ever made a decision where you just "let God" do anything? The last time I checked, we are still responsible for our thoughts, feelings and actions. Therefore, this second half is essentially communicating, "It's on you God... and if you don't do it how I see fit, then I'm not going to *let you* do anything next time." We might reason, "Let go and let God," but we are really saying, "God I'm going to let you do your thing here, but if you screw it up, you're not getting a second chance." This may not be your intent or motive when you say this, but there's an intrinsic notion to this saying that I believe strips God of His divine, glorious nature.

We must actively
pursue His Will.
We must choose to place
our trust into who
He is and what
He is capable of.

KEN SYLVIA

Instead, we must actively pursue His Will. We must choose to place our trust into *who* He is and *what* He is capable of. "Let go and let God" should really be, "Intentionally choose to submit yourself and the uncontrollable things around you to the will, desire, and purpose of God so that you might be transformed into His image through humility and obedience." But that exceeds Twitter's character limit for a single tweet. It is a far more complex relational dynamic than simply "letting go and letting God."

I also hear, "Just give it to God" quite a bit, which falls into the same category as the previous statement. There's a slight innuendo of disregarding personal responsibility and sacrifice for the sake of shifting all blame and ownership onto God. It is great if it works out, but it is then all God's fault if it does not. While the intent may be pure, it does not accurately describe the kind of life or relationship God is calling us to. Jesus did not model "just give it to God". Rather, Jesus modeled a life of intentional, disciplined trust. As I have said before, the Bible's goal is proving that God is big enough, and that He is worthy of that trust.

Two passages of Scripture speak to this issue. The first is Psalm 123: 1-2 which says, "I lift up my eyes to you, to you whose throne is in heaven. As the eyes of slaves look to the hand of their master, as the eyes of a maid look to the hand of her mistress, so our eyes look to the LORD our God, till he shows us his mercy." Psalm 124: 8 also tells us, "Our help is in the name of the LORD, the Maker of heaven and earth." These Scriptures reveal to us that there is a mysterious mixture of personal responsibility, duty, and obligation with the sovereignty and omnipotence of the Creator. Yes, God is fully in control, but He is also *not* in the business of puppet making. The Maker of the universe does not need us to maintain it, yet there is a gravitational pull for us to be engaged with Him in the process. Think about it for just a second... did God really have to use Jesus to save the world? If you think "yes", then you're basically saying God really isn't all-powerful. God in His infinite power could have done a variety of things I'm sure, but He chose His son as the best way to redeem all of Mankind.

The world did not fall apart when Jesus submitted Himself to the Father. Actually, the exact opposite happened! The world was given a second chance because Jesus, while sinless, allowed himself to be sacrificed trusting that the Father would not fail His promises. Therefore, we must take active steps across the "invisible bridge" of life. Though there are things we cannot control and cannot understand, we must actively pursue God in spite of the unknown, intentionally placing our trust in His character and ability throughout the journey. There is nothing else that will satisfy our need for security. As the Spirit reminds us in Deuteronomy 31:6, "he will never leave you or forsake you." So, allow God to be bigger than the box you have placed Him in.

MY CHAINS ARE GONE

CHAPTER 6

LIE #5: CONTROL WILL FREE ME.

I've Been Set Free

Lie #5: Control will free me

Chris Tomlin, a well-known Christian worship leader, and musical artist, composed a rendition of "Amazing Grace" in his 2006 album *See the Morning*. The lyrics go like this:

Amazing grace

How sweet the sound

That saved a wretch like me

I once was lost, but now I'm found

Was blind, but now I see

'Twas grace that taught my heart to fear

And grace my fears relieved

How precious did that grace appear

The hour I first believed

My chains are gone
I've been set free
My God, my Savior has ransomed me
And like a flood His mercy rains
Unending love, Amazing grace

The Lord has promised good to me
His word my hope secures
He will my shield and portion be
As long as life endures

My chains are gone
I've been set free
My God, my Savior has ransomed me
And like a flood His mercy rains
Unending love, Amazing grace

The earth shall soon dissolve like snow
The sun forbear to shine
But God, Who called me here below
Will be forever mine
Will be forever mine
You are forever mine

I can't help but get teary-eyed when I hear that song because there is something about freedom that touches the depth of my soul. Especially in America, there is a sense of privilege in being in the land of the free and home of the brave. There is pride and joy in knowing that we are unrestrained to pursue our dreams, practice our faith, speak out against injustice, and live without concern over being jailed or murdered over something as simple as having a different opinion. While we are definitely not perfect, we deeply value the concept of living and being free.

Freedom is a strange phenomenon though because as cliché as it is, freedom is never free. There is always a cost, and it usually requires sacrifice. In any game, there must be a winner and a loser, and the loser's prize is never as gratifying as that of first place. The winner gets to celebrate, and the loser gets to sit in reflection hoping for another chance at the top spot. If you have ever had to really sacrifice something, even for a good purpose, it can leave you feeling like you have lost.

However, this sacrifice for the sake of freedom is fortunately not a win-lose game where what is given up leaves us helpless and abandoned. Sacrificing toward freedom is a volitional endeavor. It is a deep willingness to be involved in the process. As the engine is the heartbeat of the car, the will moves us toward a greater life in freedom. The idea of being released from the chains of control gives us permission to simply be human again. It frees us up to be the *creation* and to worship the *Creator*. It allows us to walk in stride with God Himself just as Adam and Eve once did without fear, worry, or shame.

In John 10:18, Jesus says to all that can hear that no one has taken His life from Him, but that He lays it down by the authority given to Him from the Father above. This was more than just a dramatic declaration. Jesus is informing the audience, and potentially reminding Himself, that in spite of the pain, shame, and isolation He would feel, it was He who would choose to follow through. Jesus knew that surrendering His will to the will of the Father would be the key to unlocking freedom for all humanity.

Created for Him

We were not created to be in command. Nowhere in Scripture are we given absolute authority and control. There isn't even an argument to be had that Adam and Eve somehow had that authority, only to have God rip it from them and put them in extended time-out. From the onset of creation, even with the angels as we will examine later, we were made for the purpose of bringing glory and honor to the One who created us. The True Commander installed us in our respective positions to bring Himself joy by watching us carry out the missions before us.

In the spring of 2001, at 16 years old, Jesus entered my soul and changed the course of my life. As a junior in high school, I become involved in a student leadership program through the local Youth for Christ chapter. The adult leaders at the time would share about how God wanted to use teenagers like myself to change the world and be a light in the darkness on our school campuses.

I had no idea that God was preparing me for something bigger.

Upon graduating in 2003 I began volunteering through Youth for Christ in a lower socioeconomic, urban part of my city that has been known for its troubles. I worked with kids only a few years younger than myself and they gripped my heart. I saw the hurt, anger, and fear in them, but what I really saw was my reflection. God used this experience to reveal things in my heart, mind, and soul that did not reflect Himself. This process of self-examination shaped me, and He used some of these kids that I considered spiritual sons or younger brothers to help mature me. As I worked with these great young people it became crystal clear that I really wasn't as great and amazing as I thought I was. God revealed to me the depth of my need for Him.

Fast forward to 2019 where I became the Executive Director of the same local Youth for Christ. By no means is this an attempt to toot my own horn. God knows I desperately did anything I could to avoid the job. In fact, the only reason I even interviewed was because I had just undergone (my third) knee surgery, and knew all I could do is pray about the offer and seek Godly input. I even made a deal with God that if only one person said anything remotely negative, I would decline and was even prepared to seek employment elsewhere if need be because I was certain that there was no way I wanted to be an Executive Director, or that God would even call me to be an Executive Director.

Through my prayers and conversations, God not only revealed He was calling me to this position but just like that awful night alone in my house, He transformed my heart once again. Through the six-month process, God reminded me that I was created for Him, and He would be the one to direct my path. He showed me that for this time in history, it was His will for me to lead this amazing organization that my crazy, young faith took root in years ago. Although I do not know for how long He may have me here, or whether or not I'll even be that great at it, God made it abundantly clear that it was His will I use my gifts and abilities for this purpose. Ultimately, I only had two choices: trust or don't trust.

As the "boss", I now view God in a new, deeper way. Similar to how I felt when I became a dad, I now have an entirely new perspective on authority. Being a good manager, or steward of the Big Boss does not mean that we control (or own) what He has given us, nor does it mean that we are ultimately responsible for things outside of our power. As we discussed in the last chapter, it means that we acknowledge God and His Lordship, submit ourselves to His authority and then manage our lives and the things that He has entrusted to us. I see the donations, kids, volunteers, staff, policies, and I flashback to the Garden of Eden where I can only imagine Adam walked next to God naming the animals, being the Man (literally and metaphorically), but doing it as an appointed, anointed steward of the True Owner.

In my new role at Youth for Christ, I see myself as the Executive Director (for now) whose job it is to first acknowledge that I was created for Him, and put in this place for Him, by Him, under Him, surrendered to Him. Scripture teaches us to work out our salvation with fear and trembling (see Philippians 2: 12), not as pathetic dogs whose Master may whip them if they're out of line, but as reverent children who passionately desire to give the honor and glory to the One who so greatly deserves it! This, my friends, is true freedom.

If I am completely honest, there were only two reasons I did not want this job: 1) I did not want to lose what I thought I had, and 2) I did not want to be shamefully exposed as a failure. It had nothing to do with passion or calling but had everything to do with the fact that in my weakness I (still, after everything) did not see God as big enough to take an insecure person like me and use me to lead an organization seeking to transform the lives of young people. How could someone like me lead an organization seeking to transform lives, if I had not let myself be transformed to my core identity?

For His Purposes

In studying for this book, I caught onto the second part of Philippians 2:12 in a new way. The passage rolls into verse 13 and says, "for it is God who works in you to will and to act according to his good purpose." I'm not sure it would be possible to better summarize this book than in that verse. When we relinquish control over to God, actively pursuing Him, He promises to work in us for His good purpose. By taking seriously the nature of who God is and what God is through the process of working out our salvation, God opens our eyes, mind, and heart to experience His grandiosity. If we are truly saved (since

He has bought us by the blood, since His grace and our faith allow us to approach His throne confidently, and since He has given us His Spirit as a seal), then we can rest assured that He desires freedom for our lives so that we may "will and act according to his good purpose."

God has a
"good purpose" for us!
We gain freedom
by submitting to Him
and by allowing Him
to be "God" in our lives
and "beings".

KEN SYLVIA

God has a "good purpose" for us! We gain freedom by submitting to Him and by allowing Him to be "God" in our lives and "beings". This position that I am currently in as the Executive Director has been painful and challenging, yet this pain is far less than what it was like when I was lost without Jesus. The pains of this calling is worth it because I am fully confident that God wants me here, and if He has truly called me, He will not disappoint or abandon me.

In a world of confusion, however, do not misunderstand what I am trying to say. As we journey along attempting to determine God's purposes, we must practice healthy boundaries and self-control. True freedom mandates a structured value system of dos and don'ts, rights and wrongs, goods and bads. Anything other than this leads to chaos. Everyone who has been a parent or worked with kids for more than one minute knows the extreme necessity of clear expectations.

Practicing healthy boundaries and self-control provides a framework for responsibility and discipline. They force us to think and act in a way to keep us operating on the values within that framework, but also push us to realign when we violate those lines. As I discussed at the very beginning of this book, operating from a posture of holding our palms wide open keeps us humbled before the Lord. Jesus Christ modeled this perfectly in His life, death, and resurrection. His example of humility was demonstrated so we can experience freedom in a framework of trusting in God's purposes.

These temporary, earthly managerial (stewarding) positions that we were given were designed to be blessings to us, not curses. The Great Creator intended us to help manage what *He* created so that *we* could live in a constant, abiding relationship with Him. However, as we saw in the Fall of Adam and Eve, this blessing became a curse when they decided to insert their wills and desires into God's original plan. This not only kept them from God, but kept them from experiencing the freedom and excitement of seeing God's incredible capabilities when we live in His purposes.

The myth – and blatant lie – that Adam, Eve, and every human being since then have bought into is that if we can exercise our wills (or command) over the things in our lives, then we can maximize freedom. The problem with this logic is that it does not take into account any of the side effects or unforeseen consequences when we insert ourselves into the situation. As I am writing this chapter, my wife is watching *Love, Wedding, Marriage* starring Mandy Moore. It is a ridiculously cheesy movie and I reluctantly admit I watched a few parts in between paragraphs. In one of the scenes, Mandy's character – Ava – lies about her father overdosing on sleeping pills in an attempt to bring her parents back together after their recent separation. However, her unforeseen negative consequence was her husband feeling betrayed and misled in the midst of their already struggling two-month-old marriage.

This attempt by Ava to bring her parents back together robbed her of the freedom that she had with her new husband. While this example comes from Hollywood, let's look at another example from God's Word. In Genesis 15 God makes a covenant and promise with Abram (Abraham), that he, who is about eighty years old, would have a child and that through that child he would have more descendants than stars in the sky. In Genesis 16, there is a communication break down and Sarai (Sarah) convinces Abraham that the Lord has prevented her from having children and that he should sleep with Hagar, her maidservant so that she can have a family through that child. The drama continues:

> *3 So after Abram had been living in Canaan ten years, Sarai his wife took her Egyptian maidservant Hagar and gave her to her husband to be his wife. 4 He slept with Hagar, and she conceived. When she knew she was pregnant, she began to despise her mistress. 5 Then Sarai said to Abram, "You are responsible for the wrong I am suffering. I put my servant in your arms, and now that she knows she is pregnant, she despises me. May the LORD judge between you and me." 6 "Your servant is in your hands," Abram said. "Do with her whatever you think best." Then Sarai mistreated Hagar; so she fled from her.*

Any man in his right mind should know that this was going to cause problems. I can only imagine the conversation that must have *really* taken place between Abraham and Sarah. Imagine your spouse proposing the idea that you sleep with her best friend for "the sake" of having offspring. Regardless of how cute her friend might be, or whatever bribes she might offer you, the answer is a resounding... "No!" Regardless of their conversations, Abraham failed to keep his palms wide open trusting that God was big enough to give him a child in spite of modern medicine's diagnosis that he was too old and Sarah just couldn't do it. Not only did this decision cause trauma to his family, but to that of Hagar's family. However, the story does not end here, in fact, Genesis 17: 19 records that God promises Abraham that his son Isaac will be born and will provide him the descendants promised through the covenant.

Genesis 21 rolls around and the first eight verses describe the joy and ecstasy that Abraham and Sarah felt, but something happens in verse nine. The young teenager Ishmael - Hagar's son - is being silly and mocking the newborn baby Isaiah - Sarah's son. Sarah's jealousy and discontent for the servant girl and child cause her to become very upset demanding they be sent away, for good. Teenagers... right?

The truth about control is that it too often adds unnecessary pain. In both the movie mentioned above and in the story about Abraham, Sarah and Hagar, unnecessary pain was experienced because someone felt the impulse to insert their divine will into the situation. In Abraham's case, God's promise of an offspring was too much of a step across the invisible bridge, so he attempted to take control of the situation. Abraham, like Adam, failed to step up to the plate, proclaim God's goodness and truth, and stand firm upon His promises. These decisions did not just affect them, but generations to come! For those who have studied history, you will know that the Ishmaelites and descendants of Isaac (Israelites) end up warring for generations to come.

This Impacts Today

Jesus Christ came to free us and I will vehemently argue that this includes being free of the burden of control. Do you find yourself piling on extra baggage, or living humbled with palms wide open? Do you find yourself getting anxious over things that you cannot fix, and perhaps should not fix? Are you depressed just thinking about *all* the stuff *you* have to do in order to maintain the world around you? Is it worth it...? Our decisions affect our tomorrow, including the tomorrow of the next generation. If we do not take active steps toward lifting God up on His rightful place as Lord of Lords, then we by default follow in Grandpa Adam and Grandma Eve's footsteps.

Hebrews 12: 1 encourages us to "throw off everything that hinders and the sin that so easily entangles, and let us run with perseverance the race marked out for us". When we spend time trying to grab hold of the reigns of life, our focus is shifted off of the Lord's will and onto our own. I mean, if we really stop and think about it, how do we even know if the "reins" we are trying to grab are supposed to be grabbed or if they are even ours to grab? I may not have a solid theological foundation to say this with 100% confidence, but I believe that when we attempt to insert our wills in the place of God's, we sin, and this sin causes us to become entangled in a frustratingly dark place.

As I mentioned at the start of this book, I was experiencing problems with my wife because of my attempt to insert my will into her life. I was more worried about myself than I was about her in the presence of my Father. Therefore, I was not fulfilling the role that Scripture outlines for a husband. By not obeying the direction of my Father, I sinned, missing the mark that God intended for me, and to reiterate previous statements, this caused issues in our relationship. I say all of this to show that I haven't figured this out, and I do not write from a place of superiority, but a place of imperfect vulnerability. I proclaim that I am a hypocrite because just as the apostle Paul confesses, I am constantly pulled toward selfishness doing what I shouldn't, and not doing what I should (Romans 7:15).

Knowing who God has created us to be, and His purpose for our lives is vital in keeping perspective. I have observed and experienced the truth that when we attempt to exercise command over the things in our lives that are not within our creational intent or purpose, it becomes a slippery slope of "What ifs?" If *I* don't do this or if *I* don't do that then *I'll* be a bad Christian, and orphans won't eat, and the planet will die, and the whole world will implode, and we'll be forced to live on Mars (which may or may not be a practical possibility)! While I confess that is a bit overdramatic, I am trying to point out that when we overreach into God's territory, going from steward to control freak, we also take on the responsibility of being "god". We do not have the supreme knowledge and wisdom to consider the billions of factors in any given situation, so we intrinsically become overwhelmed when we step into that arena. Our duty as His creation is to know what strengths and abilities He has given us so that we can most effectively live out His purposes right here, right now.

One of my strengths, as reinforced by *Strengthfinders 2.0*, is that I am responsible. Sometimes, I am even responsible to a fault. While I have grown quite a bit over the years, I have placed a great deal of pressure on myself to live up to a certain standard, perform at a certain level, care for those I minister to, or whatever else. However, in my desire to be responsible, I can lose focus on the Ultimate Source, placing focus on myself, and causing grief and frustration in the process. It is a constant effort for me to evaluate every situation, and prayerfully consider, "God, what is Your will for me here." This has not only allowed me to be more effective in what I do but also reduce a deal of anxiety in the "What if" arena.

Choosing to acknowledge His Lordship and greatness in all situations starts a process of changing how we think as shown in Philippians 2: 12-13 earlier. For example, I can see a homeless person on the side of the road and can think... get a job... poor guy... here is a cheeseburger... glad I'm not him... or, fill in the blank. So then, the natural question in this scenario should be, "Lord, what is Your work in me so that I might fulfill Your good purpose here?" Depending on a variety of factors, our brains automatically begin a response scan that inevitably elicits various emotions. These emotional responses can lead us down a path that feels good, but that is not necessarily good. In this example, the burger may be God's will. Or, the lack of interference might prompt life change. Either way, seeking His will is mandatory because after all, we are just human.

Transformational Shift

What if we simply confessed and celebrated our humanness? What if we began to praise God for our limits? What if we began to rejoice over the fact that we cannot save the entire physical and metaphorical world? What if we worshiped God for being God, and sought forgiveness for trying to be like Him? After all, isn't that what Adam and Eve wanted... to be like God? Look what it got them. History has proven that this curse has yet to let go.

Isn't Jesus Christ the only person who has proven to be powerful enough to overcome all things, including death? Galatians 5:1 says, "It is for freedom that Christ has set us free. Stand firm, then, and do not let yourselves be burdened again by a yoke of slavery." Only God has the power to set humanity free, but only we can choose to "stand firm" and not allow ourselves to "be burdened again by a yoke of slavery." This is where I believe there is a perfect balance of honoring God and taking personal responsibility for our lives. We must glory in the fact that God paid the penalty, and that He demonstrated the power to set us free from the chains of sin, selfishness, and the craving for control. However, we must also step up to the plate with the courage to hold on to that truth, keeping our eyes fixed on the One above, and not slip back into this "slavery" Paul talks about.

Here in this context, Paul is discussing slavery in relation to our sinful nature. He is declaring to all humanity that before Christ came, died, and rose again, we were slaves to sin and its consequences. There was no power over it or hope from it. Christ, however, came and offered freedom from slavery to sin. Though we still sin, we do not have to be controlled by the sin, nor do we have to be keeping score of the sins. This is true freedom and hope that God is big enough to handle it all! We don't have to be held back by fear, but instead, we can live motivated because even in the midst of brokenness, God is the One who is in control, and He has already conquered the only thing that can keep us from Him!

The apostle Paul then instructs us in Romans 12: 2, "Do not conform any longer to the pattern of this world, but be *transformed* by the renewing of your mind. *Then* you will be able to test and approve what God's will is–his good, pleasing and perfect will." (emphasis added) First of all, Paul is telling us that we do have a choice not to give in to the world's pressures. In fact, Jesus also teaches us in Matthew 22 that the greatest commandment is to love God with our hearts, minds, and souls. He along with the people listening understood the interconnectedness of our beings. It wasn't like we were to love God only with our mind and let the rest go to Hell. No, there is – and should be – an emotional connection to our thought processes. This doesn't just impact thoughts, however, but impacts emotion. This hero of the faith is informing us of a connection between the mind and heart. In fact, when Jesus reminds us in Matthew 22 that the greatest commandment is to love God with our hearts, minds, and souls. He along with the people listening understood the interconnectedness of our beings. It wasn't like we were to love God only with our mind, and let the rest go to Hell. No, there is – and should be – an emotional connection to our thought processes.

Secondly, Paul is promising a level of life transformation because of a renewed mind. If we change how we think, we literally change how we act, and ultimately even *who* we are. Jesus says in Matthew 15: 18, "But the things that come out of the mouth come from the heart, and these make a man 'unclean.'" We develop character through transformation. Therefore, changing the process of how we think, impacts (and connects to) the emotional responses of our "hearts", and then transforms our actions and lives. For example, Romans 5: 3-4 tells us that suffering produces perseverance, and perseverance produces character, which the final product ends up being... hope. The attitude or behavior of hope is the ultimate result of a transformational shift in thinking about... suffering. That mental/emotional connection then causes us to persevere through the suffering because of an enlightened perspective about God, life, us, and whatever else.

Third and finally, Paul is concluding his logical argument with an "if, then" statement. He is ultimately saying that *if* we choose to be transformed through the process of renewal, *then* (and *only then*) will we know how to identify ("test and approve") God's will. I think it is interesting that Paul adds, "...his good, pleasing and perfect will." Is there any other kind? Is there a shelf of options? Is it like ordering at McDonald's (Chick-fil-A, let's be honest) which style of "will" we would like? Why does he throw that on the end? In my humble personal opinion, it is that Paul has gained a perspective most of us have not. After all, if anyone knows about how to have a godly attitude in the midst of suffering, it is Paul. Even as Paul writes to Timothy from jail as he is awaiting death, he expresses through his writing a tone (or sense) of peace in God's plan and will. In my own life, I have come to terms with the biblical truth that God's ways and thoughts are above my own, therefore, what might feel not-so-fun is actually part of His "perfect will." It is definitely frustrating, but experience has taught me that there is usually a visible purpose on the other side.

Having a transformative shift in thinking requires that we not only focus on the Perfect Father, but we replace the lies in our heads with His truths. The table below lists some basic examples of replacing lies with the truths of God through transformational thinking. It is not meant to be an exhaustive list by any means, but hopefully an opportunity to practice catching those thoughts and surrendering to God's transformational process.

Lie of Control...	Transformational thinking...
God can't fix this	God is all-powerful, He can do anything
Relinquishing control will cause suffering	Releasing control will grant freedom
God is good, He doesn't allow suffering	God is good, He allows all things for our good
Good decision making is enough	Renewing the mind is a start
How will I accomplish this?	God, I submit to your direction
I need to...	God, reveal what it is You are doing

The Power of Gratefulness

Thus far we have discussed the nature and consequence of believing that control provides freedom, and how shifting to transformational thinking will truly provide the peace we are looking for. However, I do not believe we have fully examined this issue until we consider the power of gratefulness. It has become widely known and accepted among psychologists that gratefulness (or the practice of being thankful) can be a magic pill in easing depression and other disorders or personal struggles, yet there is yet to be a solid scientific explanation for why or how this occurs. Well, lucky for us, the Lord provides His Divine Wisdom for this topic of gratefulness through Philippians 4: 4-8, 12-13:

> *4 Rejoice in the Lord always. I will say it again: Rejoice!*
> *5 Let your gentleness be evident to all. The Lord is near.*
> *6 Do not be anxious about anything, but in everything, by prayer and petition, with thanksgiving, present your requests to God. 7 And the peace of God, which transcends all understanding, will guard your hearts and your minds in Christ Jesus. 8 Finally, brothers, whatever is true, whatever is noble, whatever is right, whatever is pure, whatever is lovely, whatever is admirable--if anything is excellent or praiseworthy--think about such things... 12 I know what it is to be in need, and I know what it is to have plenty. I have learned the secret of being content in any and every situation, whether well fed or hungry, whether living in plenty or in want. 13 I can do everything through him who gives me strength.*

This passage is jam-packed with content, and could probably be crafted into its own book (for I am certain there's got to be at least one out there), but there are some critical points in here that we need to comprehend if we are going to unlock the treasure chest of freedom and peace. The first is simple, and we have already covered it extensively. If we look at verse four, we see that it commands us to keep God in His rightful place as the Ultimate Supreme King. Since we are the masterpiece of the Craftsman, it is counterproductive – even hurtful - to put our hope, joy, focus our effort on anything other than Him.

The second critical point is found in verses six and seven. It seems to me at least that many will recite only verse six or only verse seven, but they are really combined into one commandment. They are not stand alone in any way, rather the Lord reveals to us in verse seven that there is a peace with God to be experienced from presenting our requests to Him as seen in verse six. Here we see that Paul is declaring that the peace and freedom we are seeking can only be attained by staying rooted in Christ, the firm foundation, and taking all concerns, requests, worries, and thoughts to God *with thanksgiving*. When I think of thankfulness in this context, I view it as a vehicle or medium of transportation. Practicing thankfulness does something to us and takes us to a place that we cannot arrive at without this discipline.

I'm not a professional psychologist, but I personally view thankfulness as being *asset-based* versus deficiency-based. Asset-based says, "I have something, therefore, I can be thankful." Deficiency-based says, "I'm lacking, therefore, I am unable to be thankful." By the time Paul arrives at verse six, he has already established that as believers in Christ, we have already attained everything we could hope for. We have a relationship with the One who set the stars in place, who knows how many hairs we have (visible or not), and who separated us from predictable damnation! We literally have it all through Him who created it all, and that in and of itself should be grounds for incredible thankfulness! Yet we - definitely including me - forget to see ourselves as having this incredible richness in Christ.

The third critical point is found in verse eight and ties back into our previous discussion of transformational thinking. The Lord (via Paul) is commanding us to actively keep our minds and emotions engaged and focused on "anything that is excellent or praiseworthy". Do not get distracted with anything else, but instead only consume yourself with "whatever is true, whatever is noble, whatever is right, whatever is pure, whatever is lovely, whatever is admirable". How often do we get consumed with some grocery store magazine, sports game on TV, car parts (guilty!), neighborhood drama, or whatever else? I admit to you that I have a love (lust?) for cars. I am absolutely fascinated, and my wife just does not understand. However, there have been times where God has convicted me and has spoken, "Ken, how much closer would we be if you spent more time concerned with Me, and less time concerned with that?" I'll tell you what, that was a rather unpleasant one-way conversation.

Do we obsess over Christ? If I am completely honest, no I do not. If you have not yet been able to figure out by how I write, I do not stay focused very well. In fact, my wife makes me look straight into her eyes, turning off all other distractions as she gives me one directive at a time because I will get lost walking from the kitchen to the living room to the garage to playing something on my phone. Yet sometimes if I pause long enough, I can sense God saying to me, "Look for Me. See Me. Be with Me." God is working in my life as I write this so that even in my average day just doing my routine thing, I would look for Him, think of Him, present to Him, and keep Him in front of me just as I keep my wedding photo next to my computer.

Finally, the last critical point to unlocking true peace and freedom in our lives comes from verses twelve and thirteen. You might recognize the ever-popular, widely overused, and predominantly de-contextualized Philippians 4: 13, which says, "I can do everything through him who gives me strength." That is an amazing verse, please don't get me wrong – or stone me – because it is a powerful verse that communicates the supernatural influence of Christ in our lives. Yet, Paul only writes that in relation to verse twelve, where he informs the Philippian Church of his secret to contentment. The twelve verses preceding thirteen build to that place. So, as we look at this in context, verse thirteen speaks to being grateful regardless of our situations. In my opinion, this verse is talking more about freedom than it is everyday general life situations like athletics, shopping, or the annual eating contest!

Being grateful is a discipline in our identity. Just as we may identify with our gender, nationality, heritage, location, or whatever else, we must *be* grateful. Even if tragedy strikes, we look for the silver lining. When we cannot find the purpose of the pain, we are grateful that God is working it out and pray to be able to see His intent. If everything you have is stripped away, or if someone you love is taken, or if something terrible happens to you because of someone else's sin, then go to the One who says that you can do all things because of the strength that He gives. That is *being* grateful.

Until we discover true gratefulness, freedom in Christ will simply be a fairy tale. Start with the little things, perhaps even the everyday, simple things that we take for granted. Did you wake up this morning, and walk to your kitchen to make coffee? Did you get into your car, and drive to your job? Were you able to see where you were going, hear the birds in the air and the wind wrestle with the trees? Did you talk to any friends, whether it be with your fancy smartphone or with your voice? On your really bad days when you feel like the world is against you, are you thankful for the God of the Universe choosing to make you His special child, even when you were lost, sinful, and wanted nothing to do with Him? This my friends... is gratefulness. This is how we find freedom. This is how we see God as big enough.

THE "C" WORD: MOVING FROM ADMITTANCE TO AGREEANCE

CHAPTER 7

LIE #6: CONFESSION SHAMES US.

The "C" Word: Moving from Admittance to Agreeance

Lie #6: Confession shames us

Every year around New Year's Day people begin boasting about their new year's resolutions, or at the very least their resolutions to not have resolutions. So, as I'm writing this chapter, it is in fact New Year's Day. I find this to be quite convenient since this chapter is specifically addressing God's movement in our lives.

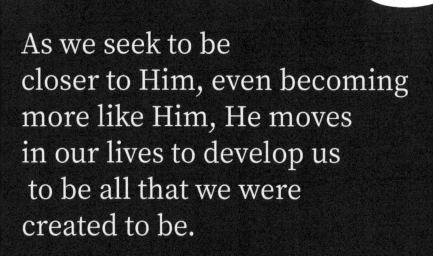

As we seek to be
closer to Him, even becoming
more like Him, He moves
in our lives to develop us
to be all that we were
created to be.

KEN SYLVIA

As we seek to be closer to Him, even becoming more like Him, He moves in our lives to develop us to be all that we were created to be. We must be careful to watch and pray for the wisdom to see the Holy Spirit moving so that we might respond in obedience and humility. Regardless of when you read this, or whether or not you are on track for your new year's resolution, I would like to challenge you with this question: Where would you like to be mentally, emotionally, relationally, spiritually in the next year? I want to leave you with that, and I challenge you to deeply consider the sacrifices and disciplines it will take to reach those goals. Perhaps you need to put this down for a few minutes to journal, plan a coffee date to have an in-depth conversation with someone you really trust, or simply keep it in the forefront of your mind as you go about your day.

Reflection is a primary function of examining our "selves", and I would argue it is impossible to truly be one in heart with the Lord without the discipline to do so. Psalm 139:23-24 says, "Search me, O God, and know my heart: try me, and know my thoughts: And see if there be any wicked way in me, and lead me in the way everlasting." Only reflecting on what is within us is not enough. For example, have you ever heard anyone brag, "Yeah I drink, but..." or "It's probably not good for me, but..."? I will admit I have made those excuses at times. These examples reveal a spiritual dissonance where one has a cognitive understanding of an issue, but fails to be transformed into a better reflection of Christ. This points to a prayer of transformation at the end of verse 24 in the above passage: "Lord, lead me in the way everlasting."

My wife and I had a dog named Nova. Nova was a very special girl to us with a personal history of how she came to be ours. She had such a unique personality, incredibly intelligent, and one of a kind. She knew exactly when it was breakfast and dinner, in fact within 30 minutes of 5 pm she would frantically let me know her biological stomach clock was beeping. She knew which beds and couches in the house she could and could not sleep on. However, one of the most curious things about Nova is that she had an incredible moral code. She knew when she had done something wrong even if we have not yet discovered what it was.

One time I came home from work a little earlier than normal, and as usual, she greeted me at the door, but something was different in this particular instance. Typically, Nova greets us with her wide array of noises, grunts, and whines, and whipping her body all over like a bull just let out of the pin while licking the air uncontrollably. However, this time was different, very different. As I opened the door and shouted out her name in excitement, I noticed the physical absence of my little boxer-mutt mix. I proceeded to say her name again, much more curiously. Finally, a little concerned, and even more annoyed that the king of the castle had not been showered with ecstatic praise, I raised my voice with a much more stern tone. This time, her brindle shadow emerged from around the kitchen counter with her tail deep between her legs, vibrating like a Chihuahua.

Of course, my first thought is, "Great, what is going to be chewed up, clawed, or broken?!" As I slowly (yet terrified on the inside because I know that I am going to have to explain whatever happened to my wife) creep into my home, one step at a time, I thoroughly examine every inch for anything out of place. First the kitchen area, then over to the living room and couches, but then, out of the corner of my eye, I notice our bedroom door is open. Making a straight dash toward the room, I cautiously peek in, expecting the worst, but hoping for the best. Shockingly, everything is in its rightful place... except for the bed.

My spoiled, ungrateful, princess of a "dog" – although I'm convinced she thought she was actually a human covered in fur – jumped up onto our (Tempurpedic) bed, ruffled the sheets, comforter, and pillows into her own private jumbo-sized, ultra-comfortable, five-star dog bed, leaving her fur and paw prints behind as evidence. This is when her so-called "sixth sense" kicked in. It was at this point I can definitively prove she heard my thoughts because as I turned around, before I could even say her name with that deep, disappointed, "you're in trouble voice", I see her cowering in the corner. With her head pointing at a 90-degree angle away from me, but with her eyes caulked all the way over in my direction, she watched my every twitch to see if she would be living in a new home that evening. The shame had set in, and she knew she was in trouble. For an animal that sometimes shows less intelligence than a rock, she knew that she broke the law before I even saw what she had done!

My dog understands what confession is. Nova knew when she and I agreed on one thing: she had done a "No, no!" Reflecting back on my earlier question at the start of the chapter, confession is a necessary element in seeing God for who He is, and how He works in our lives. However, confession at its very root is not just about "apologizing" for wrongs done but is about having an alteration of heart and mind. When I finally expressed positive emotion toward Nova, she would flail all over with joy and excitement, throwing her body around like a bull out of the gate. This was confirmation that we were once again in good standing, but of course, it did not necessarily mean that she fully understood or cared that she had been a "bad dog". Rather, she simply had an emotional response to the situation. While she will forever be one of the best dogs to ever grace this planet, it was not the last time she messed up.

Did you know that one of the primary uses for the Greek word "confess" literally means to "agree with"? On the other hand, did you know that the word "repent" (or "repentance") literally means "after mind"? Instead of just saying, "Yeah God, You're right," our minds and hearts are designed to go a step further, deeper in reflection that says, "God you're ways are above mine, You are good and great, this attitude/behavior does not reflect you, and therefore I am putting it out of sight and walking away from it entirely." God clearly cares about sacrifice, since that is what His Son Jesus did, but obedience – having an alignment of one's heart and mind with God's – is what He desires from His beloved children.

In fact, there is a clear example of this in King Saul's life as seen in 1 Samuel 15 after the Lord gives a clear instruction for him and his armies to defeat the Amalekites and completely wipe everything out in the process. Saul, in direct contradiction to the Lord's explicit command, gets this not-so-great idea to bring back all the plunder with his men to sacrifice to the Lord because apparently, he wasn't paying attention. The Lord then DMs the prophet Samuel, and the following scene unfolds as Samuel approaches King Saul:

> **19** *Why did you not obey the LORD? Why did you pounce on the plunder and do evil in the eyes of the LORD?"* **20** *"But I did obey the LORD," Saul said. "I went on the mission the LORD assigned me. I completely destroyed the Amalekites and brought back Agag their king.* **21** *The soldiers took sheep and cattle from the plunder, the best of what was devoted to God, in order to sacrifice them to the LORD your God at Gilgal."* **22** *But Samuel replied: "Does the LORD delight in burnt offerings and sacrifices as much as in obeying the voice of the LORD? To obey is better than sacrifice, and to heed is better than the fat of rams.* **23** *For rebellion is like the sin of divination, and arrogance like the evil of idolatry. Because you have rejected the word of the LORD, he has rejected you as king."* **24** *Then Saul said to Samuel, "I have sinned. I violated the LORD's command and your instructions. I was afraid of the people and so I gave in to them.* **25** *Now I beg you, forgive my sin and come back with me, so that I may worship the LORD."* **26** *But Samuel said to him, "I will not go back with you. You have rejected the word of the LORD, and the LORD has rejected you as king over Israel!"*

King Saul missed the whole point! The Lord was not asking for a sacrifice or for an apology, the God of the universe was demanding obedience. On the outside, it would have appeared that Saul was doing an amazing, selfless thing! I mean, with all those sacrifices being put to waste, he could have done a number of more profitable things with all those animals. He could have even had the most epic sacrificial event to honor the Lord leading them to victory, but sacrifice was not the Lord's expectation of king Saul. The Lord was commanding obedience, but Saul's arrogance and self-inflation, among many other things, prevented Saul from having the heart and mind of God.

Moving Toward Agreeance

Therefore, true confession must be centered on a fair, accurate, humble analysis of our obedience. If we are going to recognize God for who He is and what He is, then we must shift from simply "admitting" to "agreeing". This shift takes us from a passive place of simple observation to an active submission under God's authority. The former simply says, "Yeah, I can see where I did that." However, this requires no life-change whatsoever. On the other hand, the latter demands intentional personal change. As an example, there was once a young woman who at the time was very close to my wife and me, or at least it felt that way. She had made some unfortunate decisions and over the course of a couple hours of conversation, admitted her actions and to a certain degree even acknowledged her sin. However, there was no transformation in her heart or mind. In fact, after we had presented the truth in love, even offering support, forgiveness, acceptance, and understanding, she deliberately pushed us away. This crushed my wife and me because we knew that unless God gripped her heart, she would not be able to push through the pain of changing her behaviors. While she was cognitively aware that what she had done was wrong, she could not move toward a posture of transformational agreeance.

The process of "agreeing" requires that, as we discussed before, we renew our minds, which produces a level of transformation in *who* we are. Personal responsibility before God, self, and others is what separates passive admission from active agreement. Mind renewal is the key ingredient that helps us to truly comprehend and feel the grievances we have against the Lord of the universe. It draws us into a deeper, more intimate connection to our sin and shortcomings, and therefore, repentance takes place. Perhaps you have experienced a situation in your life when you saw the pain you had caused someone else and it so moved you that you altered (transformed) yourself in some way so that it would not be repeated in the future.

True repentance requires both a fully cognitive and fully emotional state of being, but as God created each of us in His divine, unique way we will each individually arrive here in our own way. So, we must also remember to have grace for each other in this process. For example, I tend to be much more reflective, quiet, contemplative, and take longer to really work through what is happening in my head and heart. This often means that I need a few days to work through all the thoughts racing in my mind, and emotions going up and down on the roller coaster. In contrast, others may be much more outwardly expressive, reactive, or able to more quickly process the situation.

Ultimately, we must all strive toward transformational agreeance to be obedient to the will of God regardless of our unique personality, temperament, and training.

KEN SYLVIA

Ultimately, we must all strive toward transformational agreeance to be obedient to the will of God regardless of our unique personality, temperament, and training.

As we actively seek God through relationship, trusting in His greatness and goodness becomes more natural. As one of my mentors once told me, it is like collecting spiritual data points that you can track as evidence of His presence with us. I believe this is why Jesus, the Son of God, reminds us in Luke 10:27 that the most important commandment is to "love the Lord your God with all your heart, and with all your soul, and with all your strength, and with all your mind." When we are actively pursuing the Lord with these aspects of our humanness, we collect these data points to remind us in our moments of vulnerability that He is right there with us.

Let's be honest, exposing our inner selves is terrifying. Even more so, agreeing with the truth that we have demonstrated some sort of evil or sin brings a sense of shame that can be debilitating if we are not secure in Christ. But Jesus calls us to draw near to Him. In fact, I find great comfort in Jesus's promise in John 6:37 to never cast us out of his presence if we come to him. James 4:8 also tells us that if we draw near to Him, then He will draw near to us. This demonstrates a loving, accepting Savior who will not belittle, ignore, cast aside, or tear down if we have the courage to agree with the areas that He reveals do not truly reflect Himself.

Putting it Behind

Scripture emphasizes putting sin behind us. As we looked at earlier, this is literally the basic definition of repentance. Sin of course is defined by behaviors and attitudes that miss the "bull's eye", or which fall short of God's standards. It is intentionally or even unintentionally not submitting our lives to God's plans, boundaries, and expectations. Just because we don't know it is sin, doesn't mean we aren't sinning. For example, Adam's and Eve's eyes were not "opened" until after the sin. Cain was the first murderer to ever walk the earth, even though the Sixth Commandment had not been officially written in stone (pun intended). However, once our eyes have been opened to our actions, we must choose to seek forgiveness for what we are aware of, and intentionally take steps to put those thoughts and behaviors behind us as we draw near to the Lord.

In order to really change behavior, we must have something new to focus on in order to rid ourselves of what we want to change. It is impossible to change without having a new, positive thing to keep focus on. One time – actually the only time – I went dirt-bike riding with some family members, I got a little too excited as I was starting to get the hang of it. At first, I just started out going in circles, then I would take a steep turn, then go over a little jump, but then there was this hill. The other guys would tell you that it wasn't that big of a hill, but for my first time, it was a bit of a rush. There was this one part of the hill, toward the top that required you go straight up, and make a rather sharp turn to the left. Now, once you got past that, it was a piece of cake, but missing that turn would have been a not-so-fun roll down the hill. Well, my first time up went smooth, so I became bolstered with confidence.

Being that I was pretty much a professional at this point I decided to give it some gas and be more aggressive. There was only one (probably more than one) problem this time... I lost traction on my way up and fishtailed. Now realizing I was in fact not a professional dirt-bike rider, I panicked and accidentally grabbed the throttle. Even worse, I committed the cardinal sin of dirt-biking and took my eyes off the road. Instead of looking where I wanted to go, I looked where I did not want to go, which ended up being the fence post. No matter how hard I tried to regain my focus onto the road, I just kept thinking, "Don't hit the fence post, don't hit the fence post, don't hit the... FENCE POST!" I think you can guess what happened next. That fence and I became best friends and the sweet scar on my forearm still exists to prove the toxic entanglement of our relationship.

Keeping all our attention and devotion focused on Christ is necessary for moving forward. We can never be transformed into what God is calling us to be if we allow ourselves to be distracted by the "fenceposts" of life. There will always be people, situations, and experiences that push our buttons and cause us to slip into our "old ways". Fear, worry, anxiety, pride, and shame will do all that they can to pull our attention away from Christ. The ultimate challenge is disciplining our focus on who Jesus is calling us to be, and what Jesus is calling us to do.

The apostle Paul is a great example of this and addresses this issue with the Philippian church nearly 2,000 years ago. He tells them in Philippians 3:13-15:

*But one thing I do: Forgetting what is behind and straining toward what is ahead, **14** I press on toward the goal to win the prize for which God has called me heavenward in Christ Jesus. **15** All of us who are mature should take such a view of things. And if on some point you think differently, that too God will make clear to you.*

Take a moment to re-read that passage. Consider the language Paul uses in verse 13. He acts as if the things of the past are gone, done, over with, and no longer exist, but then he clarifies his point by adding in "straining toward what is ahead." That word straining strikes me deep. Do I strain toward what is ahead? Do I *press on* toward the goal? Is every part of my being – my heart, soul, mind, strength-focused heavenward on Christ Jesus? I must admit that sometimes I am so easily distracted in other directions.

In order to put things behind us, we must keep a hawk-eye focus on what is in front of us, or just like my dirt-bike experience, those evil fence posts will keep getting in our way, and we will feel defeated and scarred. Before reading on, take some time and write down some things that you need to put behind you, and next to those things, write down opposites to focus on. For example, perhaps you struggle with this "control" issue because of various fears. You can instead focus on God, repeating the promises that perfect love casts out fear, that God is the very definition of love, and that we can confidently approach the throne of grace.

However, it would be irresponsible and foolish of me not to mention the challenge that many people have with anxiety, depression, or other issues on a daily basis. In these cases, seeking out professional counselors, therapists, and medical practitioners is vital in being able to move forward. Even having regular massages can actually allow our brains and bodies to communicate more effectively so that we can process the overwhelmingness of life. None of these should take place of a daily walk in the presence of God, but additional support can help us go deeper in our relationship with Him as we work through those daily issues. God created us to be fearfully and wonderfully made (Psalm 139:14), so paying attention to our mental, emotional, relational, and physical needs is just as important as taking care of our spiritual needs.

Job's Story

I love the story of Job because he was a good man who was a magnet for bad things and evil forces. I am in no way saying that I enjoy watching other people suffer, but Job's story is powerful. Job's authenticity, integrity, and faithfulness are nothing short of inspirational for those experiencing challenging times. In the same story, God displays unfathomable wisdom demonstrating that His vision and purposes cannot be measured. The first chapter of Job opens the story for us...

> 7 The LORD said to Satan, "Where have you come from?" Satan answered the LORD, "From roaming through the earth and going back and forth in it." 8 Then the LORD said to Satan, "Have you considered my servant Job? There is no one on earth like him; he is blameless and upright, a man who fears God and shuns evil." 9 "Does Job fear God for nothing?" Satan replied. 10 "Have you not put a hedge around him and his household and everything he has? You

have blessed the work of his hands, so that his flocks and
herds are spread throughout the land. 11 But stretch out your
hand and strike everything he has, and he will surely curse
you to your face."

Job was a man of his own kind, as this passage tells us that there was no one else like him. In fact, he was "blameless and upright". If Karma was the theological framework for this story, Job would have been on a beach sipping drinks with tiny umbrellas in a magical land far, far away. However, this is not the case and despite Job's godliness and purity, the Lord Almighty allows Satan – Mr. Scumbag of the Universe – to tempt Job into cursing the Lord's Holy Name.

Since this is not meant to be a book report on *Job* let's fast forward toward the end. After Job's friends try to make sense of all this "non"-sense, and his own wife suggests the ingenious idea of cursing God just so God Himself would strike Job dead, God turns His supernatural love and attention to Job. Job 38:1-3 tells it like this, "Then the Lord answered Job from the whirlwind: 'Who is this that questions my wisdom with such ignorant words? Brace yourself like a man, because I have some questions for you, and you must answer them.'"

Can you imagine going off on a tirade that you have the sole right to, only to be interrupted by an F-5 tornado with a voice coming from it? First of all, the sheer thought of that gives me goosebumps. Second of all, no thank you. The Lord responds to Job with a question. Almost as if to say, "Who do you think you are?" What follows is even more remarkable. The Lord then takes not only Job 38, but Job 39, all but three verses in chapter 40, and finally all of chapter 41 just to remind Job of how incredibly awesome He is. Now, let's look at Job's reply in chapter 42, verses 2-6:

> *"I know that you can do anything, and no one can stop you. You asked, 'Who is this that questions my wisdom with such ignorance?' It is I – and I was talking about things I knew nothing about, things far too wonderful for me. You said, 'Listen and I will speak! I have some questions for you, and you must answer them.' I had only heard about you before, but now I have seen you with my own eyes. I take back everything I said, and I sit in dust and ashes to show my repentance."*

What I find interesting about this story is that Job didn't do anything wrong. Job had legitimate questions and real confusion about why he was going through all the suffering. Even more interesting is that God never gives Job an explanation other than, "I am the Lord, I am the Creator... I am *your* Creator." So why did Job respond in repentance? What did he have to repent of? Simply put, Job did not recognize God's infinite wisdom, goodness, and greatness. In the midst of things, Job could neither control nor understand, he questioned God. I mean, it isn't explicitly spelled out, but by reading through the context we can clearly see Job was repentant of his attitude toward the Lord, *even though* he did *not* curse His Name.

When my son was about two years old, he contracted c-diff (a nasty intestinal infection) after a procedure. This caused him to be in intense pain, sleepless nights, stressful days, and a real test to the limits of my wife and me. To survive the next 18 or so months, we took shifts sleeping at night. It usually meant that I would stay up until about 12 pm hanging on as much as possible so my wife could sleep, then we would swap for a few hours so I could nap, and then rotate again, and again. My son would scream uncontrollably and throw his body about. Needless to say, it became quite clear how sleep deprivation and sound stimulation are used as torture tactics.

I do not remember exactly where about this journey I snapped, but one night in my weariness I cursed at God and, in my heart, I was ready to walk away. The next morning, after maybe 3-4 hours of broken-up sleep, I was still infuriated with God. I felt abandoned by Him, and I definitely felt like I had been given way more than I could bear. "Where is God in all of this?" and "Why is God putting my son and family through this?" were questions plaguing my mind. But, at some point that day, I broke before Him and just poured out my heart and soul before Him with all the thoughts and emotions swelling within me. However, I started with, "Lord, forgive me for doubting You. I was weak and I am scared, and I never really meant it. I take back what I said."

Moving toward transformational agreeance, as we have discussed, took place when I took ownership, not just for my behavior, but for putting God in a box. My problem was never God, instead, it was that God was not doing what I thought it was He should have been doing, which of course was healing my son. It wasn't God that needed to change, rather it was my definition of who God was, and how He operates.

Principles to Practice

There are some principles that we can extract from these stories that directly apply to this idea of repentance. First, we must always remember to be slow to speak and quick to listen (James 1:19). We live in a time where everything is instantaneous, social media drives us, and prestige comes with how fast you can try to make yourself sound smart. This isn't necessarily a new principle as we see with Job's friends when they jumped at the chance to share how intelligent they were (obvious sarcasm applied here). Of course, they end up looking incredibly foolish.

God has given us all a voice, and among the Body of Believers, we are commanded throughout Scripture to share our voices for the sake of lifting each other up. However, we are also warned to use caution that the words we speak are from the Lord and not our own humanistic, feel-good opinions. Take intentional time to sit quietly, listen, and allow God's presence to direct you, comfort you, encourage you, and challenge you. Even if you don't audibly hear or physically see Him, talk with Him, and not just at Him. Listening to the Lord and measuring what you think you hear against what your read in Scripture will help you to develop the skill of discernment.

Secondly, we must operate on the foundation of faith that God really is good. I don't understand how the Lord in His infinite, limitless wisdom thought it was beneficial for Satan to torment Job, destroy his property and kill off his family, but He did allow it. I mean, wouldn't *worldly* wisdom argue that this is not the evidence of a pure, holy, righteous, good God? Yet, the apostle Paul was convinced and preached with conviction that "in all things God works for the good of those who love him" (see Romans 8:28). Rewind... "in all things"! Where the world says, "God you are cruel and evil," the Lord says, "No, the Enemy is cruel and evil, bad things will happen and I can make even ashes transform into something extraordinarily beautiful!" We must take personal responsibility for the things we are able to exercise command over, but we must also choose to believe that when the Enemy strikes, God has a special purpose for that, which we may not even be aware of.

This is such a difficult mindset to adopt because in our humanistic, "us" centered world, anything that causes pain must be bad. We live in a world where everything is supposed to feel good all the time. Therefore, our world reasons that if God *allows* pain, He must be bad. However, this is not true. In fact, it is a flat-out lie from Hell. As I mentioned in previous chapters, Satan – our Enemy – only has one job description: drive us further away from the Lord. He may choose to do that through crafty lies, witty half-truths, or blatantly through theft, death, and destruction (John 10:10), but that does not reflect who God is. Even in the story of Job, consider the billions of people who have found hope and encouragement from that book.

If you are like me, however, you have hopefully already asked the question, "But what about those who are raped, tortured, murdered, orphaned, or other horrible things?" Let me be completely transparent by saying, "I don't know." It isn't fair, it isn't right, and it is *NOT* ok! In fact, I believe God's heart breaks when things like that happen. I only know two truths about life: 1) this is a messed up, evil world, and 2) God is big enough to turn any mess into something beautiful. Here are some Scriptures that help us take God out of that predetermined, finite box:

- "I have told you these things, so that in me you may have peace. In this world you will have trouble. But take heart! I have overcome the world." (John 16:33)

- "You, dear children, are from God and have overcome them, because the one who is in you is greater than the one who is in the world." (1 John 4:4)

- "...for everyone born of God overcomes the world..." (1 John 5:4)

All I know for sure is that when Christ enters our lives, the things of this world which have haunted, tormented, and damaged us cease to have power, and healing can begin through the person and work of God's Son, Jesus Christ. This does not mean that hours of counseling and therapy won't be needed, or that forgiveness will not be required, but it means that there is hope for peace and comfort in a world that cannot be controlled.

Thirdly, Godly confession (transformational agreeance) is about getting to a place of reconciliation. By admitting our sins, and then being transformed through a change of heart and mind, we are able to restore relationship with God and others. This is the proof that we aren't simply regurgitating the words we think others want to hear. Additionally, this allows us to experience freedom within ourselves. Being honest in this way empowers us to discern between the truths and lies so that we can truly be all that God desires us to be.

Finally, we must develop a pattern of prayer in our lives. Did you know that the shortest verse in the entire Bible is three words long? 1 Thessalonians 5:17 says, "Never stop praying." Some translations are only two words: "pray constantly" or "always pray". Having a mindset or attitude of prayer, by definition, forces us to acknowledge God in His position of Ultimate Power, and us in the position of being in need of that power. This behavior keeps us humble and reminds us that we – in fact – are not God. It not only reminds us of our humanness but also honors God for being The One who can bring fullness of life regardless of our situations.

As I grow closer to the Lord and more mature in my faith, however you want to define "closer" and "mature", prayer is the key factor in that process. Yes, of course, daily devotionals, "quiet times", reading positive books, listening to a good podcast from a world-renowned preacher, and a variety of other things, but prayer... it is different. It provides the opportunity to hear God's voice in the stillness. It is the vehicle the Holy Spirit uses to intercede when we can't think of the words. Prayer holds power that even Hollywood can't digitize, monetize or marketize. Quite frankly, prayer is mysterious and unseen, yet it holds the power to provide unexplainable results.

I encourage you to grab a piece of paper, journal, or the like and write down some situations in your life that seem beyond control. Start by asking God to reveal to you any area that you need to confess and repent of, and then do so. Acknowledge God's goodness and greatness, not just the things in your life that you can be grateful for, but for His character and qualities! Finally, tell Him of the things you need, the concerns and worries, the people that weigh on your heart, and the powerlessness you really feel deep down. I cannot promise immediate results, because Job's story clearly shows that the movement of God in our lives is not only individualized but unpredictable. However, I can promise you that over time – perhaps even a long period of time – God's peace will fill your life, and you will be transformed. May this journey that you are on – that we are all on – continue to progress through the power of true confession via prayer to the Great, Loving, Amazing Almighty!

WE ALL NEED
SOMEBODY
TO LEAN ON

CHAPTER 8

LIE #7: I CAN DO THIS ALL BY MYSELF, WITHOUT GOD OR OTHERS.

We All Need Somebody to Lean On

Lie #7: I can do this all by myself

More than ever, people are looking for deeper, more intimate relationships. Our world is being driven by virtual, scripted algorithms that have allowed us to be more connected than ever, but less intimate than ever. It seems there is a level of superficiality that we are all treading in, but cannot find the exit route. We are looking for ways to be engaged in a safe, trusting place where we can be accepted, share our situations and struggles, feel supported, be encouraged, and even challenged. This is why many churches are emphasizing the need for "life groups" (or some other variation of the phrase), and is also a significant reason why coffee shops everywhere are not only providers of your favorite caffeinated beverage, but also providers of casual, relaxing places to engage with others in a comfortable setting.

However, our culture is becoming incredibly polarized, politically-correct, litigious, judgmental, detached, and busy. People may be looking for ways to find relational connectedness, but without a trusted friend, don't know where to go to find it. Case in point, the next time you go out into public, watch for teenagers (and/or their parents, and/or the entire family) as they are glued to Facebook on their smartphones during dinner, walking around at the mall, or wherever else. Honestly, I am even guilty of this myself at times, especially if my wife is at Target.

I cannot tell you how many students and families I have worked with who almost exclusively communicate through texting, posts, and updates as if the entire world is unable to see their publicly displayed "private" information. I have a "friend" on Facebook (funny how in 10 years kids probably won't even know what Facebook is) who would *publicly* complain about her daughter, who also has a Facebook account by the way, and able to see everything her mother was writing about her, would then come to me to express her sadness and embarrassment. Not long ago, there was a video that went viral of a father who responded to his daughter's social media rant by shooting up her laptop... literally, shot it up. Public shaming has become a phenomenon of sorts and builds mistrust, isolates us, and causes a dysfunctional fear of healthy vulnerability with others. Unfortunately, I believe this behavior has damaged our ability to communicate and relate in God-designed ways.

As I have been in the process of writing this book, there have been countless nationwide scandals, high-profile murders, protests, and riots, increased awareness of sex trafficking, vicious elections, and more. Technology and social media have increased the average individual's ability to share their so-called expert opinions on the subject at hand, while also lacking the tact and the wisdom to do so. Recently, a close colleague of mine posted online that if "you" vote for a particular candidate, then "you" are morally corrupt and hopeless. Needless to say, I won't be having any intimate conversations exposing the depths of my struggles with this individual anytime soon. Perhaps this individual was simply joking, but like my internal reaction, how does this kind of declaration (or really attitude) positively influence others' lives? The answer is straightforward. This approach puts walls up between people and damages the potential for life-changing relationships.

Regardless of where each of us stands on these issues, I think we would all agree that people, in general, do not know how to communicate in difficult situations. I have had "friends" on social media, Christian and otherwise, who demonize and slander each other, call each other terrible names and threaten to "unfriend" their "friends" if someone else has a difference of opinion. In fact, not only have I considered doing away with the majority of my social media, but I have had numerous people tell me that they don't even bother anymore. How can we move forward, especially for those of us who call ourselves brothers and sisters in Christ, if we cannot find the resolve to love and be loved in the midst of our differences?

I am confident that when it comes to this issue of control, and journeying down the road toward God's greatness, it will only be handled in the context of loving, safe, and trustworthy relationships. Broken relationships have the greatest potential to keep us from the Light of God as they often cause us to shut down and shut out, including God Himself. Rather, God-designed relationships stretch us, challenge us, and grow us. In fact, my research in my Master's program revealed that in the backdrop of life experiences, relationships were the vital key in whether or not at-risk young people have a greater chance of deepening their faith and being successful in life.

We must learn to not only be open to others but to be the kind of people that others can be open with.

KEN SYLVIA

We must learn to not only be open to others but to be the kind of people that others can be open with. This is no easy task to accomplish without the guidance and love of the Guider Himself.

The Answer

Trust is a delicate and dynamic element. It takes time to build, develop and earn, yet it can be lost in almost an instant. Patrick Lencioni, a business expert, and consultant, wrote a book called *The Five Dysfunctions of a Team* (2002), and do you know what he discovered? Trust is the very foundation of any successful team or organization. In fact, he proposes that without this element, it is impossible to have the health that is necessary for sustainable life and growth. Even more recently, Ken Blanchard co-authored a book called *Trust Works: Four Keys to Building Lasting Relationships* (2013). Business and Leadership gurus are continually publishing works that demonstrate trust (and essentially relational connectedness) as the critical need for a productive organization.

I find it absolutely fascinating that it has taken business and leadership experts to teach us the value of trust, especially since Scripture has so much to say on the topic. I argue that the Bible is really a book about relationships. Beyond the "dos" and "don'ts", it teaches us how we are to relate to God and each other. Regardless, trust in relationships is so complex because the problem and the cure are one and the same: people. People break us, and people fix us. Therefore, we must dive into Biblical principles and lessons if we are to work toward being people that are putting each other back together.

In Matthew 22:34-40, Jesus reveals his incredible wisdom regarding this issue, summarizing the two most important commandments as relational ones:

> *"34 Hearing that Jesus had silenced the Sadducees, the Pharisees got together. 35 One of them, an expert in the law, tested him with this question: 36 "Teacher, which is the greatest commandment in the Law?" 37 Jesus replied: "'Love the Lord your God with all your heart and with all your soul and with all your mind.' 38 This is the first and greatest commandment. 39 And the second is like it: 'Love your neighbor as yourself.' 40 All the Law and the Prophets hang on these two commandments."*

Yet again, Jesus' reply to the tricky attempt of the "religious experts" was simple, yet profound. We are commanded to love God with every ounce of who we are, down to our very core. Secondarily, but equally important, we are commanded to have an equal love for others that we have for ourselves. This is exactly why surrender to God is so vital because the extent to which we do that, impacts the extent to which we are able to love ourselves, and love others. Our approach before God influences our approach before others.

Consider also what the apostle Paul shares in Philippians 2:1-5, giving clear instruction on how a life imitating Jesus Christ should look.

> *"2 Therefore if you have any encouragement from being united with Christ, if any comfort from his love, if any*

> *common sharing in the Spirit, if any tenderness and*
> *compassion, 2 then make my joy complete by being like-*
> *minded, having the same love, being one in spirit and of one*
> *mind. 3 Do nothing out of selfish ambition or vain conceit.*
> *Rather, in humility value others above yourselves, 4 not*
> *looking to your own interests but each of you to the interests*
> *of the others. 5 In your relationships with one another, have*
> *the same mindset as Christ Jesus"*

Creating a space that is "safe enough" (which is relative) for others to open up, share, and process requires hard work, not just simply obedience to a commandment. This passage boils all the fluff and distraction down to a simple principle: put others first, just like Jesus. But it is so anticlimactic! Where is the fancy psychology, hip leadership talking point, or deep intellectual thought? None of those are anywhere to be found because Paul says we are to "have the same mindset as Christ Jesus" with "humility". Reading further into verses 6 through 8:

> *"6 Who, being in very nature God, did not consider*
> *equality with God something to be used to his own*
> *advantage 7 rather, he made himself nothing by taking the*
> *very nature of a servant, being made in human likeness.*
> *8 And being found in appearance as a man, he humbled*
> *himself by becoming obedient to death—*
> *even death on a cross!"*

Jesus was unique in all that he did. He was the one human in all of history who had the ability to walk in the room and proclaim, "I'm the smartest guy here, everyone listen to how amazing I am!" Jesus literally had the ability to put anyone and everyone in their place, always being right, and always being superior. Yet, his approach to the broken was the antithesis of the religious professionals of the day, meeting people where they were at. The unlimited powers of God molded into a human frame listened, loved, extended grace, forgave, healed, gently corrected, fed, cared, and so much more. This is why even the vilest of sinners flocked to him.

God cares about our relationship with Him and with others, so much so that the bulk of Scripture is written in terms of the collective group coming together and supporting one another.

As a human species, we depend on and thrive off relationships.

KEN SYLVIA

As a human species, we depend on and thrive off relationships. Being made in God's image, He too operates in the form of the Holy Trinity: God the Father, God the Son, and God the Holy Spirit. It is through relationships we truly find the fullness of life, as God intended!

The Greatest Risk Ever

Have you ever gotten the flu, food poisoning, or some other stomach-related virus? I love to eat (just ask my wife), and the worst part of such an experience for me has been the aftershock. The residual effects make it terrifying to eat. In desperation, I'll slowly sip water and take the tiniest of nibbles off a saltine cracker. If the laws of gravity endure (i.e. everything stays down), I'll more adventurously try a full saltine, or even a small amount of canned chicken soup. After about 4 to 5 days pass, my desire to eat everything in sight will return.

Pain from broken relationships is much like the flu. The worse an illness is – or broken relationship – the harder it can be to recover. On the other hand, enduring painful experiences also present the opportunity for incredible resilience. Relationships require risk, and it does not take a genius to figure that out, but the potential reward with the right people far outweigh that risk. At some point, we are guaranteed to be let down and hurt. However, this fact does not change God's design for us to be in relationship with Him and with others. So, we have to face the fears and insecurities head-on. It is not a matter of if such trials will come, rather it is when they will come, and who will be in your circle of influence to walk with you through it.

We take risks all the time. We eat too much red meat that can potentially cause health problems, yet a fried double bacon cheeseburger with extra cheese and jalapeños sounds pretty good right about now. Driving a car is one of the top reasons people are injured or killed, yet getting into an Uber with a complete stranger makes perfect sense when it is convenient or "necessary". Every day we make decisions that are questionable at best, yet there seems to be nothing more terrifying than being vulnerable with others who have the potential to challenge our sense of worth (or being enough).

I recently sat in a workshop that talked about the role of shame in our lives and relationships. In essence, there are two kinds of shame: one says that *what you have done* is bad, causing natural guilt regarding our actions, while the other says that *who you are* as a person is deficient, bad, and unworthy, causing a distortion of our self-perceptions. The former is natural and is one of the tools God has put within us to teach us right from wrong. The latter attacks our very beings (or identity), hence why John Bradshaw calls this "toxic shame" in *Healing the Shame that Binds You.*

Toxic shame tells us that we aren't attractive enough, that we aren't smart enough, that we aren't lovable enough, that we aren't hard-working enough, that we aren't husband/wife enough, that we aren't (fill in the blank)... enough. Toxic shame affects how we see ourselves, and how we interact with others, including

God. In a strange, distorted, round-about way, shame is a version of control. Shame pushes us to do things to prove something, instead of pushing us toward Jesus. This can cause us to unconsciously (or consciously) take a certain attitude because, "Life has taught me 'this', therefore I am like 'that'." Think about the last time you did something "wrong", perhaps feeling guilty to some extent, but then immediately justifying yourself in the process? That right there is a perfect example of taking control because the feeling of inadequacy and vulnerability is too great.

Reflecting on that night as I paced in my house, yelling at the Lord, I operated on the presumption that I was not good enough or worthy enough of God's blessing. I finally had an emotional understanding of why Jacob wrestled with God: he needed to prove he was worth it. At the depth of my core, I believed I was shameful and not good enough. So, I sought to do anything and everything to quiet the shame voices. I performed academically achieving a high GPA, worked long hours, volunteered in ministry, helped others for a living, and sacrificed myself so I would earn the approval I was desperate for. Without knowing it, this behavioral pattern caused me to impose my insecurities and insufficiencies on my soon-to-be wife because I believed the lie that *who* I was, wasn't good enough.

My counselor always says that "shame is a perversion of humility." The foundation of humility is simply knowing who you are and who you are not. So, the challenge is not to avoid or perform. Instead, the challenge is to search within. The deeper we can understand who God has created us to be, the deeper we can go in our relationships with others. As the renowned Brené Brown says, "True belonging doesn't require you to change who you are; it requires you to be who you are." (https://brenebrown.com/definitions)

The greatest risk we will ever take is opening ourselves up to others, but the greatest joy we will ever experience is opening up to others. This is the intimacy that we truly desire. We can minimize that risk by knowing who we are in Jesus because he will always cover any letdowns we experience. We also maximize that joy because we know we are sharing the most truly authentic version of ourselves with others. We need others to thrive so our challenge is to find the right people who will help us grow closer to Jesus, and help us discover who he has made us to be.

The Relational Cure

"Jesus!" If you ever ask a kid in Sunday school what the right answer is, you will almost unanimously receive something to the effect of "God" or "Jesus", followed by a shout of, "Are we done yet?!" Or, at least that was my experience for a very short time as "Children's Director". It became apparent that it wasn't my calling when I had them doing push-ups, jumping jacks, and yoga before Bible storytime (at least I didn't have them play dodgeball). I think this is why I love kids so much. They are real, honest, and without reserve. They haven't been corrupted by political correctness, appropriateness, or professional expectations. Kids are raw and Jesus saw this truth in them. Matthew 19 details this amazing scene of little children being brought to Jesus. As customary for a religious teacher of the day, Jesus would pray for them, heal them and bless these little ones. However, the disciples felt that all of this nonsense with the ankle biters (again, why I didn't last in children's ministry) was a waste of Jesus's time and tried dismissing them. Jesus, on the other hand, abruptly stops them. In assumedly a stern, commanding tone Jesus replies to their lack of insight in verse 14, "Let the children come to me. Don't stop them! For the Kingdom of Heaven belongs to those who are like these children."

God has placed within us a desire to love Him and be near to Him. Yet, somewhere along the way, whether "life has taught us" or "someone told us", we learn that God is *not* good and that He is *not* really there for us. Of course, many of us would never verbalize it, but deep down, we have had our doubts. I believe the antidote for this deadly, life-robbing lie is the pursuit of childlikeness. Do not misunderstand me, for I am not saying that we should all start running around silly, having tantrums, flicking vegetables to the dog under the table, and picking our noses (although I'm not entirely sure that's reserved for children). I am saying, however, that putting ourselves in the place of a child, seeking the shameless innocence that children have, exalts God into His rightful place as a Loving, Perfect, Heavenly Father.

Now, we must address the issue of God as the Heavenly Father. Psychologists have learned that how one sees his/her earthly father directly correlates to how that same individual sees God. If daddy was violent and angry, then Big Daddy is strict, stern, and perhaps unforgiving. If daddy required performance, then Abba requires a certain level of "spirituality" before you earn His approval. In fact, many of the young people that I mentored over the years had a stunted imagination to see God as more than just an abstract idea because of their daddy's absence emotionally, physically, and spiritually.

So, let me ask you this question: "Is your relationship with God suffering because you have yet to deal with the issues you have with your earthly father, or lack thereof?" Let's go a little deeper, "Are you hurting yourself because you are not willing to forgive your earthly father and allow Abba Father to fully enter into your broken places?" I am blessed that my father and I have a wonderful relationship now, but it wasn't always like that. God has worked a miracle in our lives, and we are closer than ever, but there was a time when we didn't talk for an extended period of time.

As mentioned in the previous chapter, confession requires we examine ourselves, including the "whys" and "whats" of our lives. Sometimes it is impossible to see things in our lives because we are in the middle of our lives. A friend of mine used to say, "Fish don't know they're in water until they're not." We must accept the fact that we are flawed, broken, weak individuals and that we need others around us to maintain healthy lives. I did not begin pursuing my father until I was about twenty years old when I was encouraged and challenged to take that initial step. I am in no way promising that everything will work out like it does in the movies, but even if my father had chosen not to accept me, I still think I would have had an inexplicable peace because I know my love and acceptance was coming from God above, and was not conditional on my earthly father's response to me. I would argue that it was because I had the security of God's love that I even had the motivation to risk-taking that step with my dad.

Childlikeness is a critical key in growing closer to Christ and others because it reminds us that we are all in need. It grounds us to the truth that we are all just larger versions of kids, dependent on our Heavenly Father to provide, direct, and correct. This posture of childlikeness brings the experience of "the Kingdom of Heaven" that much closer because it invites God's presence and connects innocently with His people. Childlikeness requires that we go back to that place where we did not have to be good enough, rather we could just be. This is the relational cure, where we can just be who God made us to be, with others in this journey, accepted in His presence.

The Next Step

We need people to lean on in life. I would not be the man I am today if it was not for mentors like Toby, Marvin, Bill, Adam, and so many others in my life. Each of them encouraged me, challenged me, pushed me, held me accountable, called me out, and yes... even hurt me at times, but I never once questioned their love for me or their commitment to me. I would not have made it through the rockiest, most painful moments of my life if it was not for friends like Josh, John, Nate, and Jed who saw through my crazy, emotional self, and accepted me, but never just allowing me to stay in the muck. Equally important, counselors like Marty and Mike who sat through countless sessions with me, helping me to deal with anger, adjust my expectations, and deal with suffering in a Christ-like manner.

Let me give you some advice, be more committed to your personal growth as a human being and child of God than you are to people's opinions of you. Do whatever it takes to overcome those fears, insecurities, pains, hurts, and bad habits. Relentlessly pursue mentors, friends, counselors, and life coaches who can help you navigate the path you currently find yourself on, and who can help steer you in the right direction. Do not settle for what you have now, or be content with, "I'm OK, I'm doing all right." Be relentless in your pursuit of Christ, just as he is relentless in his love for you.

I encourage you to do an online search for local counselors in your area or ask a friend for a recommendation. Join a "Life Group" or small group at your church where you can connect, and if you can't find someone to connect with, visit somewhere you can. Not long ago, my wife attended a Bible study with a couple friends at a church she (we) didn't even attend, but where she was challenged to be more like Christ and was free to open up as the Spirit-led. I also encourage you to pick up one or more of the following books, perhaps even creating a special "book study" with some family or friends of yours:

- *Emotionally Healthy Spirituality*, Peter Scazzero

- *Boundaries*, Drs. Henry Cloud and John Townsend

- *The Gift of the Blessing*, Gary Smalley and John Trent

- *Making Peace with your Father*, David Stoop

- *How We Love*, Milan and Kay Yerkovich

- *Tired of Trying to Measure Up*, Jeff VanVonderen

- *Families Where Grace is in Place*, Jeff VanVonderen

- *Change Your Brain, Change Your Life*, Dr. Daniel Amen

- *God Distorted*, John Bishop

We need others in this journey of life. May this chapter encourage you to not procrastinate, avoid, or excuse any longer. Send that text, visit the website, make the search, and show up. Be diligent, be relentless, be motivated, and keep pressing on (Philippians 3:14).

YOU MEAN MORE
THAN YOU THINK

LIE #8: I NEED TO MAKE MYSELF MORE INSIGNIFICANT IN ORDER TO MAKE GOD BIGGER.

You Mean More Than You Think

Lie #8: We are not worth the blessing

The strange thing about experience and the psyche is that every person's neural pathways can lead to different conclusions. As I shared before, my inner turmoil about my wife led to an intense conversation (sounds way better than mostly one-sided meltdown) with God that night in my house, but this experience opened my imagination up to the possibility that I could actually be blessed by God. I had an intellectual knowledge that God loved me and cared about me, in fact, I preached that message to the youth I was working with at that time! However, that factual belief did not translate to a deep emotional comprehension. My head-to-heart connection was scrambled because my neural pathways had not yet experienced something that allowed the road to be built toward deep trust in my Heavenly Father.

Relationships in the backdrop of life experiences are what shape us, and help us to connect the dots in our hearts, minds, and souls. For example, I know that God says He would never leave me nor forsake me, but I had not yet experienced something that I could relate it to. I also know He says that He knows the hairs on my head, but so what? In the depth of my being, I needed the experience of knowing I was important to Him. Experiencing His presence that night in my house was a gift – more like an anchor – that allows me to know He is faithful to His promises. That night God showed me I am significant to Him.

Our moments of deepest exposure, vulnerability, and "nakedness" before God can be just what the doctor ordered. These are the moments we don't just understand His acceptance, but we feel it deep in our gut. Of course, they are uncomfortable, and quite frankly terrifying, but they open a door for us to let God reach into because they shine a spotlight on our deep need for Him. Isn't this why God sent His only Son to die on the cross to pay the final price of our sin? Jesus was naked and helpless, suffering so that we would have the opportunity to be in a direct unhindered relationship with Him. That is how significant we are to Him, and in Jesus's own words in Matthew 6: 25-34:

> **25** *"Therefore I tell you, do not worry about your life, what you will eat or drink; or about your body, what you will wear. Is not life more important than food, and the body more important than clothes?* **26** *Look at the birds of the air; they do not sow or reap or store away in barns, and yet your heavenly Father feeds them. Are you not much more*

valuable than they? **27** *Who of you by worrying can add a single hour to his life?* **28** *"And why do you worry about clothes? See how the lilies of the field grow. They do not labor or spin.* **29** *Yet I tell you that not even Solomon in all his splendor was dressed like one of these.* **30** *If that is how God clothes the grass of the field, which is here today and tomorrow is thrown into the fire, will he not much more clothe you, O you of little faith?* **31** *So do not worry, saying, 'What shall we eat?' or 'What shall we drink?' or 'What shall we wear?'* **32** *For the pagans run after all these things, and your heavenly Father knows that you need them.* **33** *But seek first his kingdom and his righteousness, and all these things will be given to you as well.* **34** *Therefore do not worry about tomorrow, for tomorrow will worry about itself. Each day has enough trouble of its own.*

Are these not the words of a loving, caring God? Though Jesus literally speaks of food, shelter, and clothing, he is using these items as reference to the bigger picture of life in our relationships, health, family, decisions, work, etc. Ultimately, this passage reveals that our value and worth are at the very top of God's "Concern" list.

We are incapable of accurately predicting the future, but God in His perfect, all-knowing person can. So, if God is truly concerned about our needs – emotional, mental, physical, social, and spiritual – then we should not allow ourselves to be burdened with anxiety over the issues of life, no matter how big or how small. Whether we realize it or not, or want to admit it or not, our stresses of the day are not actually about the tangible things, but about the intangible things. This is the very reason Jesus says to "seek first his Kingdom and his righteousness".

The process of pursuing God and drawing near to Him gives us perspective for the things that reach beyond our daily needs. I admit, however, this is far easier to say in a book than it is to live out in our daily lives. But it does not make it any less true or important.

I don't know about you, but the worrying, anxiety, and stress that seem to coincide with control, only causes health problems, relational tension, and a long list of other unpleasant side effects that are listed in hyper speed by the voice at the end of the commercial. I used to get so consumed with the "What ifs..." that I would forget to eat (which my wife still does not believe), would become depressed, lose weight rapidly, and have gut issues. While I have improved in many aspects, I still struggle with my sleep because I cannot turn my brain off at times. None of these things helped my situations or improved the scenarios, yet instead of keeping my eyes glued to Jesus like a teenager with an X-box, I allowed my fear of perceived control to hurt me.

Jesus points out in verse 27 from the passage above, "Who of you by worrying can add a single hour to his life?" In other words, "What good does that do?" Our worrying on things outside of our control distracts us from what is most important (and actually within our control) at the moment. So, how can we keep our eyes on Jesus and focus on what *is* within our power? Great question, Dr. Henry Cloud offers a solution to this conundrum in his book, *Boundaries for Leaders*. He suggests making two lists: one that details what *can* be controlled and another that *cannot* be controlled, and then putting all efforts into what is within our power. For example, I cannot control what the youth that I work with do, but I can control how often I pray for them, reach out to them, show support and encouragement, offer assistance, and be present in their lives.

When we are able to separate out the controllable things from the uncontrollable things, anxiety loses its grip on us. Seeking His Kingdom and righteousness gives us hope because this process affirms our volition (or our control to willingly seek Him), but also reminds us that He is ultimately the One in control. We can increase our productivity, health, and relationships by having direction on what is within our power to influence. Furthermore, if we can grasp (the head-to-heart connection) that we really are significant, then the uncontrollable things will not weigh as heavy on us. If we really do matter that much to God, then the things that trouble us – whether big or small – are also of concern to Him. So, when Jesus says that tomorrow will have its own problems, I argue that He is really proclaiming, "Your Heavenly Father is already concerned for tomorrow's happenings because He already knows what they will be. Therefore, engage in a relationship with your Heavenly Father today, because that is what will ultimately impact how you handle tomorrow!"

"But Seek First"

As Jesus wraps up his monologue, he throws a curveball at those listening. I imagine Jesus in this scene taking a dramatic pause, walking calmly over to one of his disciples, placing a hand on his shoulder, grinning with incredible joy, then looking back at the crowd, taking a deep breath, and with a soft yet God-like voice declaring, "*But* seek *first* his kingdom and his righteousness, *and* all these things will be given to you as well". Wait, that's it? That's where He leaves it! I laugh because in true Jesus fashion, he concludes his inspirational speech with a somewhat vague directive.

Doesn't Jesus know that I don't know how I am going to pay my bills this week? Doesn't Jesus see that I have no idea what to do in this particular relationship? Doesn't he see that I have this list of problems? Yes, but do we see Him? This is the point Jesus is making. He does not say that we are not to plan ahead, or consider consequences, or make tough choices, but he says to "seek first" the Father. Maybe, just maybe, Jesus is trying to remind us all that we need to let God be God. But this is so very counterintuitive! All the good leadership, psychology, and self-help books in the world have never taken this approach. When was the last time you read a book or heard a good speech, which you paid even better money for, that told you the solution to all your problem seemed entirely unrelated to the actual problem? Imagine this sales pitch, "Are you experiencing marital problems? Do you have issues at work? I have a solution for you! Avoid your spouse, call in sick, and go shopping! Learn more for 5 easy payments of only $29.95!"

The God of the universe in human flesh is spotlighting the truth that seeking His Kingdom and His righteousness is actually the solution to the problem. Our worries and control issues can so consume us that they become our idols, but by first seeking the Lord (His will for our lives, His peace, love, joy, and everything else), we become reoriented to the God who knows what tomorrow brings. We not only put God in His rightful place in our lives, but we find the contentment and peace that He desires for us to have. Jesus commands that we pursue His Kingdom and His righteousness, and in the process, all our needs will be provided for, and our worries will be calmed. Focusing on the Lord in the midst of uncontrollable chaos accomplishes what our control and worry attempt to do... put us at ease. This is the "out of the box" posture toward God, recognizing that He is big enough for every concern we have.

Jesus also introduces this revolutionary, mind-blowing, profound idea in his closing argument: every day brings its own troubles with it. Now, I realize this does not seem to be that intellectually challenging, so why does Jesus in his divine wisdom choose to end here? In my humble opinion, I think we can safely assume the obvious answer is that we forget. How many times do we wake up and ask, "Why me?", "What did I do to deserve this?", "God, are you for real right now?" So, Jesus reiterates the life-long money-back guarantee that we will have troubles. They are guaranteed, expected, and ever-present.

Let tomorrow be tomorrow,
and trust God to be big enough
for the current moment
and every future moment
here on out.

KEN SYLVIA

Therefore, let tomorrow be tomorrow, and trust God to be big enough for the current moment and every future moment here on out. As I mentioned earlier, unnecessary worry over things we cannot control has a variety of negative consequences.

Furthermore, sometimes the things we worry over don't always turn out to be as bad as we had thought. Other times, we can see that God is working out something for good even in the midst of a challenging time. Either way, isn't God still big enough to overcome? If we focus on the Lord and what we can control in the moment, then when we get to tomorrow, we will deal with that then. When we get to next week, next month, next decision, next child, next bill, we will deal with that then... and that my friends, is freedom in the present. This is the ultimate reward for seeking Him first.

Jesus is not saying we aren't accountable for our actions, instead he's emphasizing it. We are responsible to seek the Lord, focus on what we can control in the moment, and then exercise the courage to act just one step at a time. Hopefully, you can feel the freedom in that statement. We do not have to be in control of every little thing because that is not part of our earthly job descriptions as His beloved children, who He promises to provide and care for.

Stop for a brief moment and consider your specific situation. How do these "seek first" and leave tomorrow for tomorrow principles apply to your life? What does it look like for you to seek God's Kingdom and righteousness? How can you focus on God, allowing

Him to worry about the uncontrollable things around you including tomorrow's troubles? Do you really believe that you are significant enough for Him to even care? These are vital questions to consider as you and I journey closer in relationship with the Father.

Grasping the idea that we are valuable simply because we exist, that we are made in the image of God, and destined to live out our purpose of glorifying Him can be very difficult. These are all very intangible and require a great deal of faith. Quite frankly, these concepts (or beliefs) are also very challenging because they demand that we die to ourselves, removing ourselves as the idols and "gods" of our lives. We must submit ourselves to the will and direction of God, and the sin nature in us tells us this is wrong. Or, at the very least, it does not feel that great. However, if we can see that we really do mean more to God than we think – even more so than a bird or plant – then we trust that His intentions, plans, and desires for us are good and that He will take care of tomorrow's troubles.

Getting Rid of All the Junk

There was a short book written over thirty years ago by Gene Edwards called, *A Tale of Three Kings*. Though its length is not great, its depth is astounding. From different perspectives, he tells the story of King Saul's reign, then King David's reign, and followed by Absolom's uprising against his father David. The book is an in-depth examination of King David's heart and soul in the midst of Saul's attacks and Absolom's rebellion arriving at the conclusion that there is holiness in brokenness.

Whether our brokenness has resulted because of our own doing or due to someone else's bad choices, God desires a spirit of brokenness before Him. We are most aware of our need for Him when there is no possible solution to put the pieces back together ourselves. As I read Edwards's book, I wrote in the margin on one of the pages the following quote, "What if God allows us to be in uncontrollable situations to rid us of the ungodliness inside us so that He might refine us into His image?" I mean, what was the purpose of David going through everything he did with Saul? What was the purpose of my growing up in a chaotic atmosphere? What was the purpose of your... fill in the blank?

This leads us down the path toward the ultimate question, "Why does God allow bad things to happen to us?" Unfortunately, I cannot answer that question here. I do know, however, that God is good enough, big enough, and powerful enough to heal our most broken places, and to work in our lives to rid us of the things that do not reflect Him. Romans 8:28 also promises, "And we know that in all things God works for the good of those who love him, who have been called according to his purpose." As difficult as it is to fathom, God can use any pain in our lives, just like David running from Saul for years out in the desert, to mold us and shape us to reflect His goodness and glory.

I am fully convinced that God's love for us is so great that He will allow us (or as we will see, push us) to go through the crucible of suffering if that is what it takes to make us more like Him. There is a famous skit by The Skit Guys called *Chisel* where "God" pretends to chisel all the bad off of "Tommy" by using a hammer and steel chisel. Each time God chisels something off Tommy's life, he flinches, squirms, dodges, and makes excuses. This skit is a metaphor for God's desire to mold us into the masterpiece that He created us to be (see Ephesians 2:10). At one point, God tells Tommy that he is not junk because as God says, "I do not make junk." After Tommy confesses to God that he can't be good, God reassures him that he was created good, and that He loved Tommy enough to help him look more like his Creator than himself. That is a crucible experience where pain is involved in some way, *for the purpose* of forming us into a better reflection of our Creator.

As the skit shows, being chiseled, or pruned, is not one of the so-called perks we expect to receive when we sign up for this relationship stuff with Jesus. Yet, that is the number one job description Jesus gives to his followers. He clearly states the Father's desire for growth and maturity in John 15:1-6:

> *1 "I am the true vine, and my Father is the gardener. 2 He cuts off every branch in me that bears no fruit, while every branch that does bear fruit he prunes so that it will be even more fruitful. 3 You are already clean because of the word I have spoken to you. 4 Remain in me, and I will remain in you. No branch can bear fruit by itself; it must remain in the vine. Neither can you bear fruit unless you remain in me. 5 "I am the vine; you are the branches. If a man remains in me and I in him, he will bear much fruit; apart from me you can do nothing. 6 If anyone does not remain in me, he is like a branch that is thrown away and withers; such branches are picked up, thrown into the fire and burned.*

There is nothing touchy-feely about this passage. Jesus is drawing a very obvious line in the metaphorical sand. Blatantly stated, apart from Jesus we can do nothing (verse 5), and risk being cut off if we cease to bear fruit (verse 1). Furthermore, Jesus makes it crystal clear that the only way to gain access to the God of the universe is by being connected to His one and only Son. Staying connected to Jesus empowers us to do miraculous things because it is His power in us!

Chiseling, pruning, or whatever you would like to call it are unpleasant in the moment, but as the books of wisdom tell us time and time again, there are lasting benefits because of God's loving discipline (see Psalm 94:12, Proverbs 3:11-12). His love for us through the pruning experience shows that our Father desires the very best "fruit" to grow in our lives. Trusting Him through the pruning process, humbling ourselves in that place, will allow for us to grow that very "fruit" that Jesus talks about in the above passage. Paul also expands on a fruitful life in Galatians 5:22-23, "But the fruit of the Spirit is love, joy, peace, forbearance, kindness, goodness, faithfulness, gentleness, and self-control. Against such things, there is no law." Being increasingly more fruitful results from an ongoing connection to Jesus and shows the world who He is!

Pruning is an absolute necessity that we must embrace. There are no shortcuts or cheat codes that we can look up. We have to keep ourselves open to where God may lead us because it very well may be the uncomfortable means to even greater ends. It is not our tendency as humans to seek out discomfort, which means that sometimes the God who knows us better than we know ourselves (Romans 8:27) will interject – even when it does not make sense to us – because he knows we have the potential for greater fruit. You are not alone if you've ever felt like God isn't present or is allowing bad things to happen, but we must trust that even in those most painful times, God is doing something in your life to help you become all that He created you to be.

Truly understanding our significance goes hand-in-hand with the pruning process.

The greater a relationship that we engage in with the Lord – our "Abba" – the more we make ourselves available for the fiery crucible.

KEN SYLVIA

The greater a relationship that we engage in with the Lord - our "Abba" - the more we make ourselves available for the fiery crucible. This does not take place out of punishment, but out of a place of love. If trees could talk, I wonder if they would scream and cry, or if they would praise in gratitude. Would they be angry and resentful at the gardener for taking such violent and evil acts against their branches, or would they sigh in relief for having the possibilities of even greater fruit? Would they question why such evil had come against them, or would they have an eager anticipation of a greater harvest? The next time you feel like those shears are tearing you apart, remember that God has something incredible on the horizon.

A BIGGER STORY

CHAPTER 10

A Bigger Picture

It was July 18, 2014, at approximately 6:00 am that my life was about to change forever. I was startled awake by my wife's friend who informed me that my wife's water broke, and we were going to the hospital. I popped out of bed, mumbling about, frantically trying to get everything together and gather myself. I guess the rest of the day was fairly normal. We got to the hospital, checked in, heard random screams, and then waited, and waited, and waited. After about 14 or so hours, we (and by we, I mean my wife) arrived at the home stretch – literally, and metaphorically – and it would be just minutes before we welcomed our boy to the world.

Obviously, I was focused on my wife and other things I had never seen before, but during this time the NICU team came to the room. When my son finally emerged, the doctor quickly cut the cord and passed him off. I was devasted because I really wanted to cut the cord, after all, I really wasn't contributing much to the process. Also, being that this was literally my first rodeo, I was very confused. But as the NICU team began to work on my son, I realized something was very wrong.

What were only a few minutes felt like hours as time seemed to stop. "I can't find a pulse. I have no breathing!"

the nurse called out. There must have been over a dozen medical professionals in this hospital room as they tried to save my son's life. At one point, one of the nurses called out to me, "Dad, what's his name?" I stood there frozen as my exhausted wife cried and my son's body was bouncing off the table as they conducted CPR. Again, the nurse called out and I responded, "Gabriel." It was one of the top 2-3 names we had picked out, but I wasn't prepared for a decision like that under those circumstances.

As I stood in the back of the hospital room, helpless and terrified, watching everyone move like I was having an out-of-the-body experience, God spoke to me just like he did that night nearly 9 years prior. A firm, but calm voice spoke to me and said, "Don't worry, just wait and see what I do with his life." Not long after this, the NICU team informed everyone else that my son had recovered a pulse and breath, and as they moved him onto another cart to wheel him back to the NICU wing, my wife called out "Gabriel" and for a split second, opened his eyes, threw out his arms and turned to my wife. But something was still not quite right.

My son had experienced a severe loss of oxygen at some point. To this day, we still have no definitive answers as to what exactly happened, or when it happened. After two days at the local hospital's NICU, Gabriel was still not waking up, sucking, or eating, and the doctor overseeing our case informed us that he would have a high chance of having some form of cerebral palsy. We were then transferred to Stanford Children's Hospital where we stayed for just under two weeks while multiple tests were run. After an MRI on his brain revealed massive scarring and irreversible damage, the doctors informed us that the original suspicion was correct. Our son would have little to zero ability to walk, talk, or eat by mouth.

My wife and I prayed so much for our boy while he was in utero. We both felt like Gabriel would be a voice for the Lord, and prayed that God would use him, even before he was born. In fact, this is part of why the name "Gabriel" was at the top of the list of possible names since it means "strong man of God", and was the name of the angel that spoke on behalf of God. So, when we learned that Gabriel would probably never talk, I treasured in my heart the voice that said to wait and see. I had full confidence that God would answer our prayers, but I did not know in what way He would do so.

Leading up to his one-year birthday, Gabriel continued (and continues) to have multiple issues. We had countless trips to various specialists with hundreds of hours logged traveling in the car. Since his brain had been so damaged, he was very irritable at night time, so we had to take shifts caring for him and sleeping throughout the night. I personally had to balance working full time with making room to be helpful at home, often running on little sleep and being constantly emotionally drained. But in that year my wife and I had many opportunities to share our story, our hopes and fears, the lessons God was teaching us, and our trust in God's bigger picture for Gabe's life and our lives. I must have spoken to over 3,000 youth, and my wife to countless families, friends, and medical professionals during that year. Gabriel had a huge voice, but the sounds came from his parents' mouths. Of course, Gabriel has taught us many lessons since his birth, the most significant being that there is always a bigger picture when God is involved.

Changed

If we can pry our fingers off of control, then perhaps in that act (or series of acts) God can accomplish in our lives what He has been trying to do since Day One of Creation: show us that there is a bigger picture in this life now, and in life forever. Perhaps as we take a step back, the picture of life that we are desperately trying to make sense of becomes not only bigger, but clearer as His goodness and glory illuminate the screen. Maybe, as we peel off one finger at a time, we can catch a more detailed glimpse that this life we wake up to and fall asleep from really does have a purpose to it.

Significance. It is a rather dynamic and complex concept if we really take time to think about it. What defines significance? Where does it come from? Is it innate within us or does it have to be acquired somehow? I'll never forget that Friday night in March of 2001 at Cow Palace in San Francisco. I was a sophomore in high school, and God answered my prayer for significance.

I had a very unique, undeniable God-experience the year before, but it wavered after about a month or so. Reluctantly, I caved to my friends' peer-pressure, and once again attended this conference. The whole purpose of this event was to provide a hyped-up experience for teenagers to encounter Christ who may have not wanted anything to do with God. Was I "saved" at this point? I do not honestly know, but I definitely did not have the personal relationship with Him that I have now. I forget which song was being sung, but as the music pulsated through the crowd of a few thousand teenagers, I remember quieting my soul, and out of nowhere silently prayed, "Lord, I want to be important, use me."

There was not anything spectacular about this moment, nor did I have any special feeling after praying. The only other memories I do have from that weekend away are having a generally great time and coming back home a different person committed to following Christ. Honestly, I cannot even describe what else happened that caused such a 180 in my determination. Without realizing it, that one little prayer I prayed forever changed my life. It was in that moment I began the journey of submitting my identity, worth, and purpose to God. I was changed because I was asking Him to define me.

Prior to this life-altering prayer, my significance and worth was defined by *my* rules, but the change came when I asked God to be the One to define my significance *in Him*. My identity was transplanted and rooted in who Christ is, and what he did on the cross. I was no longer important because of my accomplishments, but because Christ made me important. I was special, unique, called, and adopted into a family that was all created and orchestrated by my Father in Heaven. It was no longer my athletic ability or my academic achievements that made me "special", nor was it my outward appearance, or even my amazing personality. Instead, it was the acceptance into God's Family that made me significant.

That moment – that prayer – catapulted me into a sacred place where my eyes were opened and my perspective radically changed. For the first time, I began to see my struggles, my friends and family, my choices, my own self, and everything else from a different light. I finally saw that I was a tiny part of a much bigger picture. Things that never made sense suddenly began making sense. I began to see that my pain was for others' growth, that my salvation was for others' example, and that my experiences could be for others' benefit. I was a part of a bigger picture that God had begun painting since before time began.

This transformed me because it meant that I wasn't a waste of human existence. It meant that I was not an accident and that no matter how hard I worked in life, or what terrible things happened to me, my purpose and worth were rooted in Christ and his accomplishments on the cross. It meant that God was (and still is) big enough to redeem my pride, weaknesses, and faults. It also meant that I wasn't alone in the world, and that I now belonged to the larger Body of believers around the world.

Having God's Eyes

Though it is seemingly impossible to see the "bigger picture" in the middle of this constantly developing story called "life", we still know that the bigger picture exists. Isn't this what the author of Hebrews is trying to communicate to us? Hebrews 11:1 reminds us that "faith is being sure of what we hope for and certain of what we do not see". This is the trust that God desires from us! Despite life's circumstances, we have full confidence in knowing that God is in control and is painting the perfect picture for our lives and for the lives of others that we encounter. Our inability to see the bigger picture, or know for certain God's intents and purposes, keeps us clinging to Him one day at a time.

An example of this attitude is evident in many young people we have worked with at Youth for Christ (through our Juvenile Justice Ministries program) who became incarcerated, accepting Christ while in lockup. For some of these incredible young men and women, who are facing years behind bars, hope and purpose in Christ have encouraged them to use their gifts and talents for the Lord, rather than crime. Some have taken the *opportunity* (yes, I did choose that word correctly) of being imprisoned to lead their peers to Jesus. They are conducting Bible studies, praying with others, and enduring loneliness with the knowledge that God is using them even in a dark place. This level of perseverance and endurance is impossible without the faith that God has a bigger picture we cannot yet see.

The author of Hebrews attempts to help us with this task by listing example after example of the heroes who came before us and who placed their hope and trust in an invisible God. In fact, the author reminds us that not all were privileged to see God's promises come true! The only so-called gifts many of these heroes received were persecution, torture, and being brutally murdered because of what they believed (see Hebrews 11:35-40). Yet, they stayed faithful all the way through to the end. It is almost as if the author is saying, "I know none of this seems logical, so stay connected to Him, so that you might see through the Creator's eyes! Live in wonder and awe at the masterpiece He is painting! Many people will look back at your life one day and be encouraged and empowered because of your example! So hang on because there's a bigger purpose!" This unique kind of perspective and conviction only comes when we have the faith that this brief life is only part of a much larger story, and that much larger story belongs to the Creator of The Story.

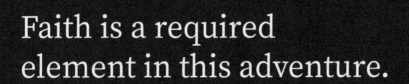

Faith is a required
element in this adventure.

KEN SYLVIA

Faith is a required element in this adventure. Chapter 11 of Hebrews uses the word faith over 20 times (depending on the specific translation) to highlight the critical attitude of the many heroes discussed. In fact, the author makes the case in Hebrews 11:6 that, "...without faith, it is impossible to please God because anyone who comes to him must believe that he exists and that he rewards those who earnestly seek him." There is this duality that on one hand, faith leads us amid incredibly difficult situations, and on the other, faith is the primary requirement in pleasing God. Furthermore, faith rests on a foundation of reward that may not even be tangibly received in this life. So, the author gives further encouragement and wisdom in chapter 12, verses 1-3:

"Therefore, since we are surrounded by such a huge crowd of witnesses to this life of faith, let us strip off every weight that slows us down, especially the sin that so easily trips us up. And let us run with endurance the race God has set before us. We do this by keeping our eyes on Jesus, the champion who initiates and perfects our faith. Because of the joy awaiting him, he endured the cross, disregarding its shame. Now he is seated in the place of honor beside God's throne."

Stop for a moment and re-read that passage. Honestly, I am torn between laughter and speechlessness because of its grandiosity. First, the author says, "Brothers and sisters, you are being watched and cheered." As if we are world-class athletes in the competition of a lifetime, we are surrounded by those who want to see us win the races that God has for us. Second, we are called to lose weight. No, I'm not talking about the extra pounds after the holidays. Rather, the author is commanding us to live like we are competing for first place. Premier athletes discipline themselves to every minute and calorie of each day to position themselves in a place where they can be victorious. Stripping off any mindset, belief, attitude, and choice is what is necessary to be at the front of the pack. Finally, the author tells us to shoot for the target by keeping our eyes on Jesus. Any competitive athlete knows the importance of focusing on what is needed to be victorious, not bothering him or herself with any distractions. Where we focus our time, efforts, and energies is where our behavioral patterns will be. So, cling to Jesus.

There is a reward for all the hard work. Enduring the pain and suffering pays off if we can keep the faith and stay focused on Him. Jesus alludes to this deeper truth in Matthew 25:23 when talking about the servant in the parable of the talents: "His master replied, 'Well done, good and faithful servant! You have been faithful with a few things; I will put you in charge of many things. Come and share your master's happiness!'" Jesus himself earned a place next to the Father's throne because of his faithfulness. Paul also tells us in Philippians 3:14, "I press on toward the goal to win the prize for which God has called me heavenward in Christ Jesus." While the reward is not tangible in our current earthly habitat, it is promised that we will receive the approval and joy of our Father in His presence.

Rewinding back to the start of this book, and of The Book, Adam walked in perfect harmony in the *presence* of our Creator. Then, He saw Adam needed a partner to look like him, and be *with* him, so along came Eve. Together, they enjoyed the *presence* of God in the Garden of Eden. Then sin happened, the world fell apart, and we were cut off from God's *presence*. But Jesus came to provide that bridge back to the Father, so that by grace through faith (Ephesians 2:8-9) we could once again be unrestricted from God's *presence*. All of history, including this present moment and all future moments to come, points us toward being free in the presence of our Father. This is the principle of seeing through God's eyes.

God so Loved the World… He Wanted to Save It

I believe the only way to summarize this book is by declaring that we are only a small part of a much larger story of which God is fully in control of, and Who has only good in mind. Our lives are paragraphs of a novel that all come together to make a masterpiece in the Hands of the Maker. Understanding that God has a bigger picture and broader story in mind allows us to be at peace with not knowing everything, not being in control of everything, and which forces us to fall at His feet in recognition of His Lordship and our humanness.

John 3:16 is a much-overused verse, but the depth of its meaning leaves us humbled and in absolute awe. The newest version of the New Living Translation translates Jesus' words like this: "For God loved the world so much that he gave his one and only Son, so that everyone who believes in him will not perish but have eternal life." However, we often stop there, failing to go one step further into verse 17 which says, "God sent his Son into the world not to judge the world, but to save the world through him." It is all about Jesus. He is the way, the truth, and the life (John 14:6). He alone makes it possible to have the hope of being in the presence of our Father.

God's strategy here will never make complete sense, at least for me. Jesus being hung on the cross and enduring the worst kind of pain and suffering known to mankind does not make sense. Was this really the only option that God could think of? I could never imagine offering up my son to be murdered for the sake of others, let alone my only son – literally. Yet, in God's infinite wisdom, He decided that this was how it had to go down. It is indescribably sobering that God had such great love for all of creation, that the only shot at redemption was through the sacrifice of a part of Himself – God the Son. It's also the point of this book, God does not fit in a box. Sometimes the things that don't make sense to us, make perfect sense to Him.

John 10:10 informs us that Christ came to give us the option for life to the fullest, now and forever. This "life" does not come to us by us "taking control", rather by trusting in the Lord of Lords and King of Kings. In all that we have discussed here in this book, the bottom line is that God is enough. He is big enough, strong enough, loving enough, able enough, and quite simply... enough. Furthermore, God shows that He wants to be more than enough for us. So, we do not need to act like God, pretending we are in control. In fact, it would be counterproductive to act that way, as we have seen.

Let us work toward allowing
God to be the Father,
and each of us being
His beloved child so that
we can find true
peace and rest.

KEN SYLVIA

Let us work toward allowing God to be the Father, and each of us being His beloved child so that we can find true peace and rest.

This is seeing God outside of the box...

"All things have been committed to me by my Father. No one knows the Son except the Father, and no one knows the Father except the Son and those to whom the Son chooses to reveal him. "Come to me, all you who are weary and burdened, and I will give you rest. Take my yoke upon you and learn from me, for I am gentle and humble in heart, and you will find rest for your souls. For my yoke is easy and my burden is light." ~Jesus, Matthew 11:27-30